The Canterbury Book of
New Parish Prayers

The
Canterbury Book of
New Parish Prayers

*Collects for the Church and
for the World*

M. J. Kramer

CANTERBURY
PRESS
Norwich

First published in 2020 by the Canterbury Press Norwich
Editorial office
3rd Floor, Invicta House
108–114 Golden Lane
London EC1Y 0TG, UK
www.canterburypress.co.uk

Canterbury Press is an imprint of Hymns Ancient & Modern Ltd
(a registered charity)

Hymns Ancient & Modern® is a registered trademark of
Hymns Ancient & Modern Ltd
13A Hellesdon Park Road, Norwich,
Norfolk NR6 5DR, UK

Concluding Texts and Seasonal Blessings from
Common Worship: Services and Prayers for the Church of England
© The Archbishops' Council 2000.
Common Worship: Times and Seasons
© The Archbishops' Council 2006.

British Library Cataloguing in Publication data

A catalogue record for this book is available
from the British Library

978-1-78622-303-6

Typeset by Regent Typesetting
Printed and bound in Great Britain by
CPI Group (UK) Ltd

*This book of prayers is dedicated to
all who have suffered and died
in the COVID-19 Pandemic and
to all who have cared for them.*

Contents

Introduction

The Purpose of this Book

One of my responsibilities as the Precentor at Canterbury Cathedral is to lead the prayers at Evensong every day. When I looked for resources to assist with this ministry, I found that classic prayer collections often now sound dated in both style and subject matter, and that many contemporary published prayers were too lengthy, and too intimate in tone, to be used effectively in a public context. This led me to write my own collect-style prayers for Evensong each night, and these prayers, prayed here day by day in this Mother Church of the Anglican Communion, provide the core of this collection.

The purpose of this book is to enable you to find, with the minimum of effort, a bidding and a prayer for a wide range of topics. It is ideal for those leading public worship, school assemblies and public meetings at which prayers are offered, and I hope it is also of use to people who wish to include formal prayers in their times of personal reflection.

The pages that follow contain prayers for the seasons and festivals of the church year, aspects of the Christian life, and the needs of the Church and the world. The collection covers topics familiar from older prayer books, such as the unity of the Church, peace and social justice, but also includes a range of prayers on subjects that have come to the fore in more recent years, such as evangelism, the environment, mental health and the challenges of combatting prejudice and discrimination in our society. The style is contemporary but relatively formal, enabling the prayers to fulfil the traditional role of collects, collecting into one the intercessions and meditations of the people.

Using this Book to Lead Others in Prayer

This prayer book aims to make the lives of those who pray a little easier, and so I encourage all who use it to adapt the biddings and prayers to their own needs in whatever way they wish. For those who are new to leading prayers in public, there is some guidance provided below, and some suggestions for how the book might be used to support private prayer.

Selecting from the prayers

The first principle in leading formal prayers is that they should be brief. At a service of Evensong, I would tend to limit myself to two prayers. At a school assembly or a public meeting, a single bidding and prayer may well be enough. On a very special occasion, where a number of topics need to be addressed (for example when someone is taking on a new role, or when a group is leaving the community), three might be used. If more than this are read on a single occasion the amount of words used, and the repeated nature of the collect form, make it hard to maintain the prayerful interest of those who have gathered. The combination of a small number of prayers together with moments of silence is often far more effective than a mountain of words, however beautifully composed.

The second principle is striking a balance between prayers for the Church and prayers for the world. One of each is a good solution, and the division of the prayers between Parts 2 and 3 of the book encourages this balanced approach. On feast days, or in particular church seasons, the special prayers provided towards the front of the volume are a good starting point, and a number of them are cross-referenced to a complementary prayer that speaks to a need in the world. At other times, the readings set for the service, the nature of the act of worship, particular concerns of the local church or community, or current affairs may well suggest which sections of this book to explore.

The third principle in selecting prayers is ensuring that a variety of needs are being addressed in intercessions over time. A casual look down the list of Contents may be a helpful reminder of topics that have not recently been addressed in prayer, and may help those leading worship to avoid the temptation simply to repeat what has become a hackneyed list of concerns.

Leading the prayers

Preparation

For those new to leading prayers, it is ideal to read the chosen biddings and prayers out loud in private before doing so in public. This enables the reader to get the flow of the sense correct, and also to jot down any additions or changes that are desired. This preparation will enable the prayers to be delivered with confidence and fluency, and help those listening to concentrate on what is being said, rather than the way it is being delivered.

Structure and silence

When leading the prayers themselves, the ordered combination of bidding, silence and collect is key. Beginning the time of prayer with words as simple as 'Let us pray', followed by a short silence, sets the mood immediately and gives people the opportunity to settle their bodies and their hearts into a state in which they can attend to what follows. Once the atmosphere has settled, the bidding can be read.

The biddings provided form a starting point for those leading prayers, or a backup option in case of a lack of inspiration, but they can easily be altered or expanded to include any local, topical and personal details relevant to the situation. It is, however, important in doing so to be mindful of brevity to continue to hold the focus of those at prayer.

Following the bidding, a short silence allows those assembled to reflect on what has been said and to add in silence any personal intercessions the bidding has suggested to them. These personal prayers are then gathered together in the words of the collect, to which those gathered respond, with encouragement from the leader if necessary, 'Amen'.

After the prayers have been completed, the time of prayer may be concluded by everyone saying together the words of the Our Father, the Grace, another form of words that is appropriate in the context, or by the giving of a blessing. These standard texts are provided at the back of this book for those who prefer to have the words on hand.

Use of the voice

Really effective use of the voice in leading public prayer only comes with experience. However, a few aspects of vocal production are worth considering when leading prayers for the first time. The crucial issue is that prayers must be audible and clear to all those who are gathered. Prayers that cannot be heard or understood because of issues of volume, speed or diction are best left unsaid, and prayers that hover around the edge of audibility are intensely distracting, as they require those listening to concentrate not on prayer but rather on reconstructing what they might have missed. If the place has a microphone system, it is worth having a practice in advance, but it is also worth remembering that the acoustics will often be very different when the space is filled with people, and so there is always a need to be aware of how audible the prayers are as they are being led 'live'. It is also useful to request (and attend to) constructive feedback from a trusted friend or colleague.

As a ministry of leading prayers develops, reflection on other aspects of vocal delivery is also helpful, although the key is always that the end product sounds natural. In terms of speed, it is necessary to speak slow enough to allow for prayerful 'space' around the words, while also keeping the flow of the sense clear to avoid any slowness of speech sounding mannered or distracting.

Another aspect is that in leading public prayers the officiant is speaking *for* the people to God, rather than speaking *to* or *at* the people. The voice of the leader needs to be heard as a voice that comes alongside people, rather than a voice directed towards them. This requires a different tone from a sermon, a greeting, a lecture or a reading, and it is worth exploring how this can sound natural in each voice. I find that what comes naturally to me in leading prayers is to speak in a slightly lower and more consistent pitch, with a little less attack in the consonants than I would use when preaching, while all the time working to maintain volume, clarity and audibility.

Using this Book for Personal Prayer

There are many spiritual practises that can help guide and deepen the life of personal prayer, yet one of the challenges often remains simply getting started. Here the structure of biddings and collects in this book may offer some assistance.

After settling into a prayerful position and frame of mind (maybe using material from the section on Prayer, p. 92), select a prayer for yourself, the Church or the world. Read the bidding to yourself and then, in silence, allow yourself to reflect on the topics for prayer the bidding introduces. You might add areas of concern not mentioned in the bidding; you might personalize the bidding by thinking of particular individuals or situations in your life that the bidding touches on; you might be led to explore aspects of your own behaviour and the ways you can support those you are praying for.

When your reflection seems to come to a natural end – it is better not to force it to continue longer merely to meet a time target for prayer – close with the words of the collect. You can then move on and use this book to explore other topics for prayer, depending on the time you have available. At the end you could finish with one of the concluding prayers at the back of this book.

Acknowledgements

I owe an enormous debt of gratitude to all those who have encouraged me at Canterbury by telling me of their appreciation for my prayers, and particularly to those enthusiasts, like the Revd Professor Kathy Grieb, who have (repeatedly!) urged me to collect them together into a book. I wish to record my thanks also to Canterbury Press for accepting this volume, which I hope will make the lives of many clergy and laity a little easier for some years to come, and to Christine Smith, Rachel Geddes and Mary Matthews, who have helped me with aplomb through the publication process. I owe so much to Mrs Hilary Fairhurst, who not only read through the original manuscript but has been the best Music and Liturgy Administrator a Precentor could hope for, and to my friends in the Dean and Chapter, the Choral Foundation, and the Cathedral staff, who have made my ministry at Canterbury such a delight.

These prayers were collected together during the national lockdown imposed in 2020 because of the COVID-19 pandemic, and it is to all those who have suffered and died from that disease, and to all who have cared for them, that this book is dedicated.

PART I

The Church Year

Advent

Advent – expecting Christ's presence to come and knowing it in our lives today

Lord, we pray for your Church, that in this Advent season we would hear ever more profoundly your call on our lives.

Almighty God,
as we rejoice in your Son's first coming,
so we await with eager expectation the fulfilment of his promise
that he will come among us again.
Strengthen us in our faith,
that we may know his presence with us in our daily lives,
and fashion our souls to be places where his coming righteousness
    will be at home,
through the same Jesus Christ our Lord.

Advent – longing for Christ's coming

Lord, we pray for your Church, that through this Advent season we may await with joy the coming of your Son.

God of glory,
whose Son looked on the brokenness of this world in love,
and in his mercy came to bring us healing and peace,
grant us grace to long for his coming again,
that our hearts would be opened by his compassion,
and our world would be reconciled by his inspiration,
through the same Jesus Christ our Lord.

Advent – personal transformation (the prophets)

Lord, we pray for your Church, that we would open our eyes to
your light in our world and open our hearts to be eager for your
coming kingdom.

Lord our God,
through your prophets you comforted us in our weakness
and called us to use our strengths for the good of others.
As we pray in this season for Christ's coming,
so we ask that we would have the confidence to renew our
    own lives,
that, through compassion and practical service,
we may be made agents of your kingdom in our world,
through Jesus Christ our Lord.

Advent – seeing Christ's presence in our world

Lord, we pray for your Church, that we would be awake to your
presence in our worship and in our daily lives.

Lord God,
as we prepare our hearts to receive your Son,
give us his humility, that we may know him in the lives of others;
give us his honesty, that we may speak out against all that brings
    cruelty and violence;
and give us his joy, that we may come to know this whole world
    as your gift,
that in all that we do and say
his presence would be made known
and his name glorified,
through the same Jesus Christ our Lord.

Advent – the two comings of Christ

Lord, we pray for your Church, that our eyes would be opened to
the coming of your Son in this Advent season.

Heavenly Father,
at his first coming your Son was born in obscurity,
and he calls us now to be awake and watchful for his coming
    again in glory.
Open our eyes, and the eyes of all people, to see his action in
    the world,
through the offering of worship,
the transformation of lives
and the sharing of love,
through the same Jesus Christ our Lord.

Advent – waiting in worship

Lord, we pray for your Church that through our Advent journey
we may be filled with expectation, and glorify you in the beauty
of our worship, the depth of our prayer and the devotion of
our service.

God of gods,
whom saints and angels worship and adore,
as we prepare our hearts for your Son's coming,
renew our spirits with the joy of your hope,
that reaching out to you in our waiting,
and praising you in our worship,
we may come to know more deeply the mystery of Christ
and the fullness of your divine compassion on our world,
through the same Jesus Christ our Lord.

Advent – Gaudete Sunday
(The Third Sunday of Advent)

Lord, we pray for your Church. As we keep today this Gaudete
Sunday, and hear once again the command to rejoice, so we pray
that all Christians would be filled with joy and hope as we await
with eager hearts the coming of your Son.

God of joy,
you rejoice in the unity of the Son and the Spirit,
and you take delight in all you have made.
In this Advent season teach us to share in your joy,
that in times of sorrow, as in times of happiness,
we may come to know the reassurance of your promise
and the fulfilment found in coming to be fully alive,
radiant with your glory and charged with your hope,
through Jesus Christ our Lord.

Advent – The Great O Antiphons

Advent – O Sapientia (O Wisdom)

Lord, we pray for your Church. As we enter this last part of
Advent, we pray with eager hearts for the coming of the Lord
Jesus in our prayer, in our shared worship, in our relationships
and in all aspects of our lives.

Lord Jesus,
you are the wisdom of God,
with whom, in the beginning, the Father and the Holy Spirit
    fashioned the world.
Come to us this day
and grant us a share of that wisdom,
that we may know what is right, what is holy and what will bear
    good fruit,
for ourselves, our society and the whole world,
for you live and reign with the Father and the Holy Spirit,
one God, now and for ever.

See also Wisdom (p. 301)

                                             Part 1 The Church Year

Advent – O Adonai

Lord, who appeared in the burning bush to Moses, we pray
for your Church, that in all we do we may be granted a clearer
knowledge of your presence with us, and your power to
transform our lives.

Lord God,
in the burning bush you made known to Moses your Sacred Name
and promised to be with him always.
Help us to encounter you more profoundly in our common
    worship and our private prayer,
that we may come to know more deeply the mystery of your being
and the call that you have on each one of our lives,
through Jesus Christ our Lord.

See also Justice – gift of the law (p. 178)

Advent – O Radix Jesse (O Root of Jesse)

Lord God, whose Son stood as a sign among the peoples, we
pray for your Church, that we may bear witness to Christ both in
favourable times and in times of difficulty and oppression.

Lord God,
your Son Jesus Christ
stood as a sign of self-giving love that contradicts
the pride and the aggression of this world.
Help us, who are formed in his image
and redeemed by his sacrifice,
to bring all the nations to faith in you
and to show all peoples the justice and compassion of
    your kingdom,
through the same Jesus Christ our Lord.

See also Oppression (p. 182)

Advent – O Clavis David (O Key of David)

Lord, whose Son is the Key of David and the sceptre of the House
of Israel, we give you thanks for the roots of our faith among the
people of Israel, and pray for your Church, that we may promote
harmony between all faiths in word and action.

Lord Jesus Christ,
you were born of the line of David,
and a star's rising revealed you as king of the Jews.
Teach your Church your own gentleness and understanding,
that we may learn to live in love and cooperation
with people of all faiths and none,
that together we would work towards a better future for our world
and greater insight into the mystery of God,
for the sake of your holy name,
O Jesus Christ our Lord.

See also Justice – prisoners (p. 179)

Advent – O Oriens (O Morning Star)

Lord, who came to bring light into darkness, bring your clarity
and hope to your Church, that in the darkness of doubt and
confusion we may find the light of faith and love.

Lord Jesus Christ,
you are the morning star that scatters the darkness from before
    your path;
bring to light, we pray,
all that will lead us in ways of truth.
Where we deceive ourselves,
show us the reality of our characters and circumstances;
where we deceive others,
renew our consciences to speak with honesty and compassion;
where we are deceived about you,
show us the reality of your love and your will for our lives;
for the sake of your glorious name,
O Jesus Christ our Lord.

See also Those in need – Advent and Christmas (p. 249)

Advent – O Rex Gentium (O King of the Nations)

Lord God, whose Son came among us to save the human race, which you created in the beginning and which you will bring fully to yourself in the end, we pray for your Church, that we may preach to all the nations your loving purposes of salvation.

Lord God,
out of whose love we were made in the beginning
and through whose love we are redeemed in Jesus Christ,
be with us in all that we do,
that inspired by your creativity,
stirred by your compassion
and empowered by your Spirit,
we may bring to the waiting world the message of salvation,
through words of truth
and deeds of love,
in Jesus Christ our Lord.

See also Peace – shared humanity (p. 145)

Advent – O Emmanuel

Lord, whose Son Jesus Christ came as Emmanuel, God with Us, we pray for your Church, that we may live out our vocation in the consciousness of his presence with us in each moment of our lives.

Lord God,
your word was made flesh and came to dwell among us
and lives for ever as the hope of the nations.
Renew within your Church the gift of hope,
give us the vision to dream of a better future,
the courage to work to bring it about
and the steadfastness to resist cynicism and despair,
that through your Son's presence
we may know that great things are possible
for all who believe in his name,
that is Jesus Christ our Lord.

See also Hope – urgent hope for the coming of Christ (p. 294)

Advent – O Virgo virginum (O Virgin of virgins)

Lord, as we begin our celebrations of the Christmas feast, so we pray for your Church, that like Mary, the Virgin of virgins, we may be obedient to your call on our lives.

Lord God,
whose servant Mary was marvellously called to be the mother of
  your Son,
give us her spirit of wisdom and faith,
that we may lay aside all doubt and selfishness,
and follow that path that you have laid before us
in confidence and in joy,
through the power of Jesus Christ our Lord.

See also Motherhood – mothers (p. 213)

Christmas

Christmas – God with us

Lord of all, we pray for your Church, that renewed by the great mystery of Christmas, we may live out our faith in love and in joy.

Almighty God,
whose Son Jesus Christ is Emmanuel, God With Us,
help us to know his presence among us
and to be so transformed by his power,
that in our worship, our words and our actions
we may reflect something of the glory
of the light of the world
to those with whom we share our lives,
through the same Jesus Christ our Lord.

Christmas – the coming of the light

Lord, we pray for your Church, that enlightened by the light of Christ we may share that light with others.

God of light,
in you there is no darkness at all;
shine, we pray, your light into the darkness of our lives,
that we may know the truth of ourselves,
that we may bring healing to places of division and conflict,
and that we may see the path that you have set before us to walk in,
through Jesus Christ our Lord.

Christmas – sharing the light of Christ

Lord, we pray for your Church, that inspired by the coming of Christ in Bethlehem we may offer ourselves as light in all this world's places of darkness.

Heavenly Father,
we give you thanks that your Son,
with whom you made the heavens and the earth,
came among us as a child in the manger of Bethlehem
to bring us light and life and hope.
Be with us, we pray, in our journey through life,
that we may share his love with others
through lives lived in joy, friendship and generosity,
through the same Jesus Christ our Lord.

Christmas – Christ as child, teacher and crucified

Lord, we pray for your Church, that through our words and our deeds the truth of your mystery would be known in all the world.

Loving God,
you reveal yourself to us
in the child in the manger,
the teacher in the temple
and the man on the Cross.
Open our eyes, that we may know more of your truth,
that we may experience more of your love
and that we may share more of your joy in the world,
through the same Jesus Christ our Lord.

Christmas – Christ draws all to himself

Lord, we pray for your Church, that we may have the love and the faith to seek you in our everyday lives.

Heavenly Father,
whose Son Jesus Christ
was adored by kings and shepherds,
was followed by tax collectors and fishermen
and was preached by visionaries and outcasts,
strengthen us in his service,
that in our day, his love would draw together people of all races,
    nations and classes
as one family in your service,
for the sake of the same Jesus Christ our Lord.

Epiphany

Epiphany – revelation of Christ to the world and to each one of us

Lord God, as we celebrate the feast of the Epiphany, Christ's glorious appearing to the world, so we pray for your Church, that through our words and by our deeds we would reveal your glory in our lives.

Light of lights,
Jesus Christ,
before whom the sages from afar bent the knee and offered gifts,
show yourself in our hearts this day.
Give us the love to seek you,
the humility to worship you
and the courage to speak of you to others,
for you are our God indeed,
O Jesus Christ our Lord.

Epiphany – the splendour of his coming

Lord, as we glory in the radiance of your Son, we pray that we may make him visible to the world through the integrity of our lives.

Lord of all,
the glory of your Son is made manifest
in the homage of the magi,
the voice from the heavens
and the miracle of the water become wine.
Help us, who dwell in the shadows of this changing world,
to see the light of his eternal splendour,
that we may be faithful in worship,
fervent in proclamation
and joyous in his company,
through the same Jesus Christ our Lord.

Epiphany – water into wine

Lord, we pray for your Church, that filled with the new wine of
the kingdom we may bring joy and inspiration to our world.

O God,
whose Son Jesus Christ, as the first of his signs,
made water into wine at Cana of Galilee,
pour out on your Church the overflowing gift of your Spirit,
that our hearts would be strengthened,
and our lives would be transformed,
by the knowledge that you have created us for joy
and have called us to share with you in the eternal banquet
   of heaven,
through the same Jesus Christ our Lord.

Baptism of Christ

Lord, we pray for your Church. Strengthen us in the freedom and
power of our baptism, that we may bring your light to our world.

God of all creation,
in the beginning you fashioned the waters to be a source of life,
and in the coming of your Son you sanctified them anew
to bring us the fullness of life that is found in him;
strengthen all the baptized in the service of his gospel,
that we may minister to the world
his healing, his forgiveness and his love,
through the same Jesus Christ our Lord.

Candlemas

Lord, we pray for your Church, that we would be filled with the
light of Christ in all that we do.

God of all nations,
whose servant Simeon saw in the child Jesus the revelation of your
   ancient promises,
and whose servant Anna spoke of his truth to all who were
   seeking redemption,
stir up within us your gift of faith,
that our eyes may see our salvation in Jesus Christ
and our lives be turned to his service,
in words of conviction and deeds of compassion,
through the same Jesus Christ our Lord.

Lent: Penitence & Forgiveness

Lent – forgive our weaknesses

Lord God, have mercy on your Church, that we may serve you
with pure hearts.

God of compassion,
you keep on loving us when we go astray,
and in your gentleness call us back to yourself.
Have mercy on us when we fail you
through cruelty or laziness or lack of self-control,
and as you forgive us, help us to forgive ourselves
and to dedicate our lives to your service and the service of others,
through Jesus Christ our Lord.

Lent – penitence

Lord, we pray for your Church, for forgiveness for those times
when we have failed to show your love, and for encouragement in
our renewed efforts to bring your light to the world.

Gracious God,
you are slow to anger and rich in mercy;
in this season of penitence,
show us where we have strayed from your love.
Teach us the meaning of true repentance
and bring us back to your generous heart,
that we may serve you and our neighbours
with the freedom of those who know that we are ourselves
    loved by you,
in Jesus Christ our Lord.

Lent – purify our hearts

Lord, we pray for your Church, that in this holy season we would
be purified of all corruption and serve you with clean hearts.

Lord God,
healer of the broken,
lover of the sinful,
raiser up of the fallen;
in this season of Lent direct our hearts,
that leaving behind all that distracts us,
and turning to you in prayer,
we may come to know you as our most attentive listener
and may come to know our true selves with honesty and
    with compassion,
in Jesus Christ our Lord.

Lent: Growth in Grace

Lent – a season of honesty

Lord, we pray for your Church, that we may be transformed by
the light of your love.

God of truth,
you know all our actions, our words and the thoughts of
    our hearts;
teach us to be honest with you and with ourselves,
bind up that within us which is broken,
calm that within us which is disturbed
and transform that within us which has gone awry,
that our souls may be filled with the gentleness, the justice
    and the joy
that we have come to know in Jesus Christ our Lord.

Lent – growth in knowledge of God and self

Lord, we pray for your Church, that through this Lent we would
be led to deeper truths about you and about ourselves.

Creator of all,
you brought this world into being from nothing
and sent your Son into it, to redeem it at the cost of his life.
May we, who in this holy season commemorate his sufferings
    for us,
be brought to understand something of the depth of your love,
from which not one of us can be separated,
in Jesus Christ our Lord.

Lent – take from us all that is cruel

Lord, we pray for your Church, that you would hear us with love
and guide us with gentleness.

God of compassion,
in whose love our life is renewed,
our faith is restored
and our service is strengthened,
open our hearts this Lent to your transforming call.
Take from us all that is untrue,
all that is selfish,
all that is cruel,
and fill us with your kindness,
that our hearts of stone would become hearts of flesh,
rich with possibility for the creation of a better world,
in Jesus Christ our Lord.

Lent – let us seek God and resist temptation

Lord, we pray for your Church, that through Lent we may be
brought to a deeper understanding of you and of ourselves.

God our light,
in your gentleness
you guide us on the path through life,
until we come at the last to the rest of your eternal home.
Strengthen us on this our journey through Lent,
that we may steadfastly seek you,
courageously resist temptation
and grow in that love which brings
comfort to others and fulfilment to our souls,
through Jesus Christ our Lord.

Lent – a season of transformation

Lord, we pray for your Church, that throughout this Lent we would be guided by the promptings of your Spirit.

God our inspiration,
you call us in the midst of our lives
to reach out beyond ourselves to new possibilities and fresh hopes.
In the journey of this season of Lent,
give us the openness to hear what you might be saying to us,
and the humility to be transformed into our truest selves,
loved from all eternity,
in Jesus Christ our Lord.

Lent: Pilgrimage & Guidance

Lent – guidance through the season

Lord, we pray for your Church, that you would guide us on our journey through Lent.

Almighty God,
whose holy people journeyed through the desert
and whose Son Jesus Christ was driven into the wilderness,
be with us as we make our sacred pilgrimage through Lent.
Refresh us with the living waters of prayer,
feed us with the spiritual food of the Scriptures,
protect us from the heats of life's temptations
and bring us at the last
to your promised land of plenty, rest and joy,
through the same Jesus Christ our Lord.

Lent – pilgrimage

Lord, we pray for your Church, that we may be renewed and
transformed by our journey through Lent.

God of our pilgrimage,
by whose light alone the path before us becomes clear
and by whose hope we are given the confidence to continue in
    the way,
bless us through the journey of our lives,
that in all our strivings, our plans, our disappointments and our
    new beginnings,
we would know your presence as our companion,
and come to understand, ever more deeply,
that unconditional love offered to us in your Son,
Jesus Christ our Lord.

Lent – wilderness

Lord, we pray for your Church, that through this season of Lent
you would lead us more deeply into your love and teach us more
of your truth.

God our guide,
in the wilderness we hear your voice,
and when we are lost you come to call us home.
Direct our steps on this journey of life,
take from us the lies of self-deception
and the apathy that enables us to turn aside from others' pain,
and bring us to a knowledge of your love
so deep that we can dwell there with both honesty and peace,
through Jesus Christ our Lord.

Mothering Sunday (The Fourth Sunday of Lent)

See Our Welcome (p. 76) and Motherhood & Pregnancy (p. 213)

Passiontide & Holy Week

Passiontide – companionship of Christ in suffering

God of all, we pray for your Church, that we may know Christ's presence with us in times of suffering and in times of joy, in times of hope and in times of despair.

God of love,
whose only Son took on himself the weight of all
    human suffering,
that in our times of struggle we would know we are never alone,
shine your light into our hearts,
that in all our confusion we would know your guidance,
in all our despair know your hope
and in all our loneliness know your friendship,
in the same Jesus Christ our Lord.

Passiontide – the cost of love

Lord, we pray for our Church, that transformed by the power of the Cross we may be renewed in compassion and inspired with the hope that all suffering is at the last enfolded in the life of your love.

Heavenly Father,
whose Son Jesus Christ came to show us what it means to live out
    of love,
and to reveal to us its price in this our broken world,
strengthen us in our pilgrimage of life,
that we may offer ourselves completely for others.
Take from us all selfishness
and the insecurity that leads us to attack others to feel
    safe ourselves,
and make our hearts open, compassionate and free,
through the power of his sacred heart,
the heart of Jesus Christ our Lord.

Passiontide – the mystery of the Cross

Lord, we pray for your Church. As we keep the season of
Passiontide, we pray that as we meditate on the Cross of Christ
we may come to know, amid his sufferings, his love and his glory.

God of love,
whose only Son did not refuse the pain of suffering and death,
and who embraced the Cross for the freedom and redemption of
    the world,
may we, who seek to follow in his path,
grow in understanding of this sacred mystery,
and through its power
grow in strength, thankfulness and hope,
through the same Jesus Christ our Lord.

Passiontide – transforming sorrow into love

Lord, we pray for your Church, that we may learn to lament.
Teach us to know and share in the griefs and sufferings of our
world, that bearing them with Christ, we may share in his divine
work of transforming sorrow into love.

Lord Jesus Christ,
on the Cross you bore the whole weight of this world's suffering,
the whole weight of this world's cruelty,
the whole weight of this world's despair,
and yet, in accepting such sorrow, you transformed it into love.
Strengthen us, who are your disciples,
to participate in this great mystery,
that we might offer compassion in a world of selfishness,
reflection in a world of hasty actions
and reconciliation in a world in which people exploit divisions,
that the power of your Cross would be known in our lives
and the glory of your deathless life would be known in all
    the world,
O Jesus Christ our Lord.

Passiontide – preparation for Holy Week

Lord, we pray for your Church. As we spend these final few
days preparing to enter into Holy Week, we pray that you
would inspire our hearts afresh to draw close to you at this most
sacred time.

God of all,
whose Son Jesus Christ
walked the path of suffering love to the end,
renew our spirits as we prepare to walk with him over the days
 that lie ahead.
Give us seriousness of intent,
give us compassion of heart
and give us openness of mind,
that all we hear, do and say
may transform our souls and reinvigorate our lives,
through Jesus Christ our Lord.

Passiontide – sharers in Christ's sufferings and Resurrection

Lord, we pray for your Church, that strengthened on our
pilgrimage through life we may walk in the law of the Lord.

God of creation,
whose only Son absorbed the violence and cruelty of this world
and by his compassion transformed it into love,
grant us the grace in our sufferings to share in his passion
and in our joys to share in his Resurrection,
that, grafted into him,
we may be inheritors of a life
that is free, that is true and that is holy,
through the power of the same Jesus Christ our Lord.

Passiontide – unite our sufferings with Christ's Passion

Lord, we pray for your Church, that through the contemplation
of Christ's sufferings we may grow more deeply into his love.

Lord Jesus Christ,
who for us endured the pain of the Cross and the mockery of
    the crowd,
bless us as we follow in your way.
Unify the sufferings of our lives with your Passion,
that they may bear fruit for our souls in ever deeper kindness
and ever richer humanity,
that through them we may be empowered
to show the world something of your love and gentleness,
for the sake of your glorious name,
O Jesus Christ our Lord.

See also Pain – the Passion of Christ (p. 253)
and Carers for loved ones who suffer – Mary's care for Jesus in his
Passion (p. 257)

Palm Sunday

Lord, we pray for your Church, that we may greet our Lord with
joy and have the courage to follow him to the Cross.

Lord Jesus Christ,
the crowds acclaimed you as king
yet later called for your death;
your disciples followed you in life
yet so many of them abandoned you at the last.
Help us in our weakness to follow you on our journey through
    this sacred week,
that we may keep our eyes fixed on your Passion
and through it come to know the glory of the hope of
    the Resurrection,
which you hold out to all who follow you,
O Jesus Christ our Lord.

Holy Wednesday

See Betrayal – friend of betrayers and betrayed (p. 230)

Maundy Thursday – a new commandment

Lord, on this Maundy Thursday we pray for your gift of love,
that we may know your love of us and that we may show love to
one another.

Lord God,
whose Son Jesus Christ commanded us to love one another,
take from us all greed, envy and pride,
that by showing gentleness to all those we meet
we may open their eyes to the transformative love that has been
    shown to us
in the same Jesus Christ our Lord.

Maundy Thursday – the gift of the Eucharist

Lord, on this day when your Son shared his last supper with his
disciples, we give you thanks for the gift of the Eucharist. Grant
that, feeding always on the spiritual food of his body and blood,
we may be strengthened in our vocation to be the body of Christ
in our world.

Lord Jesus Christ,
you offered your life for our salvation on the Cross
and you offer yourself to us anew each day in the sacrament of
    your body and blood.
Deepen us in our love for your Eucharist,
that strengthened by your presence
we may serve you in a world
marked by the same pain, betrayal and suffering that you knew,
for the sake of your glorious name,
O Jesus Christ our Lord.

Good Friday – salvation is accomplished on the Cross

Lord, on this day when our Lord Jesus Christ laid down his life
for the world, we pray that in looking on his Cross we may know
both the cruelty of this world and your eternal love.

God of Glory,
whose Son Jesus Christ offered up his life that the world
    might live,
fix our eyes on his Cross,
that in the Crucifixion of our Saviour we may know
the depth of this world's sin and the perfection of your
    forgiveness,
the pain of this world's hurt and the comfort of your healing,
the fragility of human life and the promise of its eternal destiny,
through one who was lifted high to draw all people to himself,
even Jesus Christ our Lord.

Holy Saturday

Lord God, as on this Holy Saturday Jesus lies in the tomb, so we
pray for your Church in all its uncertainties and perplexities, that
we may know the hope of life to come and the guidance of Christ
our King.

God of all,
the earth is hushed,
and all creation waits in stillness
while your Son lies in the tomb.
Direct us in our earthly journey,
that we may experience by faith
that hope which as yet we cannot see:
the hope that death's word is not the last
and that the end of all truth
is life everlasting and the fullness of communion with you,
in Jesus Christ our Lord.

Easter

The Easter Season

Lord, we pray for your Church, that in this Easter season we may
have the faith to know our Lord as risen indeed.

O Lord Jesus Christ,
through your rising again hope has been renewed,
joy has been restored
and life has been re-created for this whole world.
Give us grace in this season of celebration
to rise to you in our hearts,
that with prayer and song we may re-echo
that hymn of joy which your Easter began,
O Jesus Christ our Lord.

Easter – keeping a holy Eastertide

Lord, we pray for your Church, that together with the whole of
creation we may rejoice in the Resurrection of Christ.

God of creation,
in love you brought this world into being
and in mercy you called it to new life in your Son;
bless Christians throughout the world as we celebrate this
    Easter Feast,
that it may be for us
a season of encouragement,
a time of thanksgiving
and an inspiration to bring the gospel to others,
through the same Jesus Christ our Lord.

Easter – Resurrection brings light to the world

Lord, we pray for your Church, that filled with the joy of your
Son's rising, we would proclaim the truth of the Resurrection to
the whole world.

God of Glory,
your Son's rising fills the world with light
and your people's hearts with joy.
In the exultation of this holy season,
drive from us the darkness of despair and confusion,
that we may live all our days
in the power of the victory over death
of your Son, Jesus Christ our Lord.

*See also The dying & all who await the Resurrection with longing
(p. 236)*

Ascension

Lord, we pray for your Church. As we celebrate Ascension Day,
we give thanks that, in returning to the glory of heaven, your Son
opened for us a way to your presence.

King of glory,
whose Son was raised into the heights of heaven
and sits at your right hand to reign over all,
grant us your grace,
that inspired by this vision of hope
we may find the confidence to do your will
and the freedom to offer our whole lives in your service,
in Jesus Christ our Lord.

Pentecost

Pentecost – may the Spirit breathe on us afresh

Lord God, we pray for your Church. Renew the gift of your Holy Spirit on us, that set free from our defensiveness and pride we may come to love you and one another with honesty and vulnerability.

Holy Spirit of God,
wind of inspiration,
fire of language,
guardian of truth,
breathe anew on your waiting Church.
Refresh within our community your many gifts,
that seeking out love with patience, genuineness and commitment,
we may be re-formed each day
into the glorious body of the eternal Son,
Jesus Christ our Lord.

Pentecost – the Spirit moved on the face of the waters

Lord, we pray for your Church, that with willing spirits and hearts aflame with love, we would speak of your truth with conviction and with gentleness.

God of all,
in the beginning your Spirit moved on the face of the waters
and brought life and breath to all creation.
Send your Spirit on us this day,
that renewed in zeal,
deepened in prayer
and strengthened in confidence,
we would show the world the meaning of a love that has
    no ending,
in Jesus Christ our Lord.

Pentecost – the gift of the Church and its renewal by the Spirit

Lord our God, we thank you for all the blessings that we receive
at your hand through the Church, for the beauty of worship,
the inspiration of teaching and the joy of knowing you in our
daily lives. Refresh us with your Spirit, that each day we may be
renewed in our praise and in our service.

Lord of glory,
you speak to us through your Scriptures, your creation and your
    songs of praise;
pour down the riches of your grace on your Church
and bring new life and animation to all that we do.
When we are tired or careworn,
inspire us again with the excitement of the life of the Spirit,
that we may love you, praise you and proclaim your truth
to souls that yearn to hear words of pardon, peace and hope,
through Jesus Christ our Lord.

Pentecost – inspiration for evangelism

Lord, we pray for your Church, that on this day of Pentecost we
would be filled anew with the fire of your Holy Spirit.

Holy Spirit of God,
you descended on the apostles in tongues of flame
and enabled them to speak the good news of Christ in all the
    languages of their hearers.
Breathe on us afresh we pray,
that enlivened by your inspiration
and strengthened by your power,
we may speak of the hope that is in Christ to those around us
in ways marked by generosity, conviction and creativity,
through Jesus Christ our Lord.

Pentecost – inspiration for service

Lord, we pray for your Church. As we thank you for the gift of
Pentecost so we pray that, renewed by the Spirit's life, we would
do Christ's work in our world.

Lord of all life,
your Holy Spirit brings hope in despair,
joy in sorrow,
energy in despondency
and life in death.
Stir up our hearts we pray, that by the Spirit's power
and strengthened by the encouragement of one another,
we may bring your love in service to a world
so much in need of your light and your warmth,
through Jesus Christ our Lord.

See also Peace through dialogue (p. 149)

Trinity Sunday

Trinity Sunday – celebrating life in relationship

Lord, we pray for your Church. As we celebrate Trinity Sunday,
we give thanks that the heart of God is revealed to us as
relationship and love.

Lord God,
at the heart of whose being is relationship
and whose truest name is Love,
be with all those who seek to live out that love in your world.
Give us courage to reach out to those different from ourselves,
give us discernment in building relationships with them
and give us compassion to know their joys and sufferings as
    our own,
in Jesus Christ our Lord.

Trinity Sunday – the Trinity as a model for life in the Church

Lord, we pray for your Church. As we celebrate Trinity Sunday, we pray for the unity of the Church, that just as the Trinity is one, so we would be one in faith, hope and love.

God of truth,
your very self finds its unity in the joy of love,
a love in which you have called us all to share.
In your mercy, draw all those who follow you into that harmony
    for which you long,
that treasuring our rich diversity of gifts and traditions,
and sharing them with openness and generosity,
we may offer to you in unity
that one true sacrifice by which the world is reconciled
    with heaven
and all creation is made new,
in Jesus Christ our Lord.

Trinity Sunday – make us anew in your image

Lord, we pray for your Church, that strengthened in the faith of the Holy Trinity we may proclaim your love to all those around us.

Lord God,
Three in One,
in whose unity we see the image of love made perfect,
strengthen us all in our human loves,
that with you as our inspiration and our goal
we may preach the good news of the possibilities of a
    different world
to a humanity torn apart by our jealousy and selfishness,
that all things would be made new,
in Jesus Christ our Lord.

Trinity Sunday – seeing the Trinity in our lives

Lord, we pray for your Church, that with our vision transformed by the contemplation of the mystery of the Holy Trinity, we would see the pattern of your life of love in all things.

Lord of vision,
whose prophets saw the truth of your majesty
shot through the truth of this world,
reveal to us something of your glory and your action in our lives,
that knowing you as love's deepest reality
we may come to enjoy that love's bright reflections
in those around us, in the splendour of the natural order and in
    the silence of prayer,
through Jesus Christ our Lord.

Corpus Christi

As we celebrate Corpus Christi, the day of thanksgiving for the Eucharist, so we pray for greater understanding of the Eucharist throughout the Christian Church. And we pray that by sharing in one bread, the whole Church may be, ever more visibly, the one body of Christ.

O God,
through the power of the Cross you have called us into the
    mystical body of your Son.
Help us, who feed on the bread of life in the Eucharist,
to be drawn more closely to you through the Spirit,
to discover our unity more profoundly with one another
and to share your generous love with those with whom we share
    our lives,
through Jesus Christ our Lord.

Ordinary Time – First Sunday after Trinity

Lord we pray for your Church, that enlightened by the glory of
the Holy Trinity we may bear God's light to our world.

Holy God,
in your light we see light,
and through your mercy we discover the meaning of truth,
   beauty and love.
Bless us as we begin this season of growth,
that as the plants bring forth the loveliness of flowers and the
   sustenance of food,
so our spirits may bear rich fruit in words and deeds that are
   delightful in your eyes
and that help to support all those who are in need,
through Jesus Christ our Lord.

Harvest Festival

Harvest Festival – the harvest of the Lord

Lord of all, we pray for your Church, that we may take our part
in sowing the seed of the gospel in our land and serve you in
gathering in its fruits in good works and lives transformed.

God of the whole world,
whose Son taught us that the harvest of the kingdom is plentiful
but the labourers are few,
send us out, we pray, to work for your harvest.
Show us where your Spirit is at work in our world
and where its fruits are ready to be gathered in;
teach us how best to tend and nurture the gifts and faith you have
   given to others;
and reveal to us your plan for our society,
that we may work towards its fulfilment,
gathering a harvest of good things to prepare the banquet of
   the kingdom,
where all shall eat and be satisfied in your presence,
through Jesus Christ our Lord.

For Harvest and Rogation see also Farming (pp. 264–6)

Christ the King

Christ the King – Christ as child and king

Lord, we pray for your Church. As we celebrate the feast of
Christ the King, renew our spirits we pray, that trusting in Christ
alone, we may have the confidence to face all the challenges of
this life.

Lord God,
your Son came to us as a child
yet lives and reigns in heaven as a king.
Through his example,
and with the aid of his Spirit,
help us to know the power and promise of our own vulnerability
and the true origins of our strength and talents,
in Jesus Christ our Lord.

Christ the King – rule in our hearts

Lord of Lords, we pray for your Church, that we may be found
faithful to the pattern of life shown to us in your Son, the King
of Glory.

Almighty God,
who exalted your only Son to be king of all,
rule in our hearts this day,
that we may be cleansed from our habitual worship
of human power and status, riches and popularity,
and serve you alone, the one true God of love,
through the same Jesus Christ our Lord.

*See also Leaders – grant them the virtues of a true leader (p. 162)
and Social justice – a fairer world (p. 180)*

Festivals & Observances

Our Lady

Heavenly Father, as we give thanks for the witness of the Blessed
Virgin Mary, we pray that we may have confidence to follow, like
her, the path you lay before each one of us.

Lord of all,
in your grace you chose Mary to be the mother of your Son,
and in your wisdom you prepared her with the gifts of faith,
    hope and love.
Strengthen us in your service, we pray,
that we may discover within ourselves the resources you have
    given us
to fulfil our vocation in life,
and that we may have the confidence, the trust and the compassion
to follow where you lead,
through Jesus Christ our Lord.

Our Lady – Mary's 'yes'

Lord God, we pray for your Church. On this day when we celebrate
the Blessed Virgin Mary we pray that, inspired by her example and
aided by her prayers, all Christians would lead lives of openness to
your call and have the confidence to say 'yes' to your will.

God of glory, who chose Mary to be the one
whose motherhood would bring forth the Saviour of the world,
grant us your grace that, learning from her faithfulness,
strengthened by her courage and delighted by her joy,
we would offer our whole lives in dedication to your service,
bearing Christ to all those we meet,
through the same Jesus Christ our Lord.

The Apostles

Lord God, as we celebrate the feast of N, so we pray that, like
him, we might have the courage to offer our whole life to Christ.

Heavenly Father,
at the call of your Son, N followed,
not knowing where that call would lead and not counting
   the cost.
Grant to us and to all Christians, we pray,
his openness to hear your call,
his courage to persist in adversity
and his love to desire nothing more than friendship with you,
through Jesus Christ our Lord.

Evangelists

Lord, we pray for your Church. As we give thanks for the witness
of N in his writings, so we pray that we may preach the gospel of
Christ not only in our words but also through our lives.

O God of glory,
whose truth is known in the writing of the Evangelists
and in the teaching of the Church,
grant us the grace
to be so captivated by the depths of this truth
that as we give thanks for those who have led us to the light,
so we too may bring to the lives of others
a glimpse of the splendour of your radiance
and a reflection of the warmth of your love,
through Jesus Christ our Lord.

Martyrs

See The Persecuted Church (pp. 65–6)

Teachers of the faith

See Students – learning throughout life (p. 282)

The Calendar

The Naming & Circumcision of Jesus (1 January)

Lord, as we give thanks for the Naming and Circumcision of your Son, may each one of us come to know his love more deeply, and our own self more honestly.

God our Creator,
you fashioned us at our beginning
and in you alone is the secret of our purpose revealed.
Direct us in our journey through this life,
that as we come to know more profoundly the person of Jesus,
so we may discover more truthfully our own identity in you
and our own value in your eyes,
through the same Jesus Christ our Lord.

St Basil the Great & St Gregory of Nazianzus (2 January)

See Teachers (p. 284)

St Agnes (21 January)

For St Agnes and other martyrs, see Equality – forced marriage (p. 292)

The Conversion of St Paul (25 January)

Lord, we pray for your Church, that strengthened by the example
and prayers of St Paul we would proclaim your name to the whole
world.

God of truth,
who brought Paul, through encounter with Jesus,
to be a messenger of your love,
guide our steps as we journey on the path of life,
that we may know that your love is for all peoples without
    distinction
and have the courage to preach the same,
through Jesus Christ our Lord.

See also Violence – perpetrators of violence (p. 192)

Holocaust Memorial Day (27 January)

Father of all, on this Holocaust Memorial Day we remember
before you all those who lost their lives in the Nazi persecution
and all those many genocides where intolerance has led to
violence. We pray for an end to prejudice throughout our world,
a renewed commitment to the dignity of each human life and a
determination among all people that the lessons of the past would
be remembered and taken to heart.

God our Creator,
you know the power of human beings to do good
and our power to wound;
you know our ability to bring healing
and our readiness to turn to violence.
Hold in your love, we pray, all those who have suffered and
    suffer still
the cruelty of others' words and others' hands,
and change our hearts,
that we may see in others not enemies and competitors
but brothers and sisters, fellow children of the same
    Heavenly Father,
in Jesus Christ our Lord.

Ethelbert, King of Kent (25 February)

See Ordained ministry – supporters and encouragers (p. 88)

St Joseph (19 March)

On this day when the Church celebrates the example of Joseph, husband of the Blessed Virgin Mary, we pray that, like him, we would know patience, understanding and courage.

Lord God,
at the Incarnation of your Son
your servant Joseph listened in obedience to your word,
and through patience supported his family in a situation he could
   not fully understand.
Be with us and all Christian people,
that we may learn to bear with one another,
to encourage one another in the faith
and to support one another
through all the changing circumstances, emotions and
   convictions of this life,
through Jesus Christ our Lord.

St Joseph – a faithful servant of Christ (19 March)

Lord, we pray for your Church. As we celebrate St Joseph, so we pray that, like him, we may be found faithful servants of Christ.

God of love,
who strengthened Joseph to share with Mary in caring for the
   infant Christ,
give us your compassion for those in need,
that we may long to serve them,
and grant us your wisdom and strength,
that we may be enabled to do so with judgement and constancy,
through the same Jesus Christ our Lord.

*See also Work – encouragement and purpose in our labour
(p. 277)*

St George, Patron of England (23 April)

Lord, as we give thanks for the bravery and witness of St George
our patron, so we pray that, filled with his strength and his
courage, our nation would continue to flourish in service of one
another and of our world.

Almighty God,
whose soldier, St George, fought for the faith
even at the cost of his life,
inspire us with his commitment and his fortitude, we pray,
that, striving for what is right
and shunning what is corrupt,
we may be found to be faithful warriors for the cause of love,
through Jesus Christ our Lord.

See also The persecuted Church (p. 66)

St Mark (25 April)

Lord, we pray for your Church. As we glory in the writings of St
Mark, we praise you for the teaching we have received, and pray
that we may hand it on with faithfulness and love.

Lord Jesus, Son of God,
whose faithful servant Mark proclaimed the great mystery of your
    coming among us,
and told of your participation in all the joys and sorrows of our
    human life,
take from us all narrowness of vision and coldness of heart,
that we may know how much we still have to learn of your truth
and be open to the emotions through which you so often teach
    us to love,
for the sake of your holy name,
O Jesus Christ our Lord.

St Philip & St James (1 May)

Lord, on this day when we remember your apostles Philip and James, we pray that the Church may be true to their legacy of faithfulness, seeking after truth and bringing others to Jesus.

Lord Jesus Christ,
whose apostles longed to hear your words of spirit and life,
and who worked to bring those words to others,
renew your Church in our day,
that inspired by their example and aided by their prayers
we may be renewed in our desire for you,
refreshed in our mission to the world
and restored in our bodies, minds and relationships,
through Jesus Christ our Lord.

Saints & Martyrs of the Reformation (4 May)

Lord, as we remember on this day all those who struggled and suffered on both sides in the upheavals of the Reformation, we pray for your Church in our time. May we be informed in our faith by the questions they raised and the convictions they held, and may our sorrow at their suffering lead us to seek ever greater unity within the Church, and ever greater understanding between Christians of different traditions.

Lord of all,
whose reality is greater than any one mind can conceive
and whose love is more perfect than any one heart can express,
as we recall both the insights and the pain of the Reformation era,
renew our commitment to one another in our shared striving after
   the truth of the faith;
that working together in unity
we may discover more deeply the truth of your nature
and the meaning of the purposes you have for us,
through our shared teacher and Saviour,
Jesus Christ our Lord.

Julian of Norwich (8 May)

Lord, on this day when the Church remembers Julian of Norwich,
we give thanks for her insight and pray that like her we, together
with the whole Church, may be led to a deeper vision of your
infinite love.

God our Mother and our Father,
God our light and our hope,
you hold the whole of creation like a hazelnut in your hand
and look on it with nothing but love.
Strengthen us in this life,
that we may resist the seductions of envy, pride and violence,
and look on one another with your eyes,
as those loved into being human and liked into becoming whole,
in Jesus Christ our Lord.

See also The sick (p. 254)

St Matthias (14 May)

Lord, we pray for your Church. As we remember Matthias, on
whom the lot fell to take on the authority of an apostle, so we
pray for all those stepping into new positions of authority in our
Church at this time.

Lord of the Church,
we thank you for the richness of the faith we have received at the
    hands of our forebears,
for their guidance and their wisdom,
for their nurturing and their gentleness.
As you call others to take on their responsibility through the
    passing years,
sustain them with your grace,
that they may deliver to the next generation
that which they themselves received:
the gospel of the love of God and the hope of the life eternal,
made known to us in Jesus Christ our Lord.

St Augustine of Canterbury – Missionaries (26 May)

Lord, as we recall the mission of Augustine to the peoples of this
land, inspired by the vision of Gregory the Great and nurtured
by the welcome and support of Bertha, Queen of Kent, we pray
for all those who preach the gospel throughout our world and all
who strengthen them in their work.

God of all,
whose gospel is gone out into all lands
and whose word is made known to the ends of the world,
we give thanks for the faith established anew in our land
by the mission of St Augustine of Canterbury.
May we who follow in his footsteps
bring the truth of Christ to the people of this nation,
and may all who follow his pattern of missionary life
find strength in your presence with them,
and welcome wherever they go,
through Jesus Christ our Lord.

The Visitation of Our Lady – The Magnificat (31 May)

Lord, we pray for your Church. As the joy of the Incarnation led
Mary to share her gladness with her cousin Elizabeth, so may we
be led by joy to proclaim Christ's coming to a waiting world.

God our Saviour,
the Incarnation of your Son brings joy to our spirit
and blessing to our world.
In your eternal mercy, show your strength in our lives.
Lift up the lowly and scatter the proud,
fill the hungry with good things and send the rich empty away,
that this world may reflect ever more closely
the pattern of your kingdom of justice and peace,
made known to us through your promises to our ancestors
and inaugurated in your Son,
Jesus Christ our Lord.

See also Motherhood – pregnancy (p. 214)

Part 1 The Church Year

St Barnabas (11 June)

Lord, we pray for your Church. As we celebrate St Barnabas, the son of encouragement, we pray for the gift of encouragement in our Christian life, that through offering encouragement to one another and receiving it ourselves, we may be strengthened to serve as we are called.

God of love,
your vision for our lives is greater than we can imagine
and your ability to enable us to achieve it is larger than we dare hope.
In your gentleness,
grant us your gift of encouragement,
that looking with kindness on all that is within us,
our strengths and our weaknesses,
our talents and our failings,
we may know the path you have laid before us
and be granted the confidence to follow it to the end,
in the company of Jesus Christ our Lord.

The Birth of John the Baptist (24 June)

O God, we pray for your Church. As we rejoice in the birth of John the Baptist, so we pray that, inspired by his example, we may preach your gospel to a world thirsty for truth.

O God,
John the Baptist proclaimed that your kingdom was close at hand,
and called us to turn away from all that keeps us far from you.
Grant us your mercy,
that we may search our souls in honesty,
repent of all that holds us back from your love
and welcome that wonderful transformation that you prepare to
    work in us,
that by the power of your Spirit we too might be heralds of
    your kingdom
and live in the joy of your company,
through Jesus Christ our Lord.

See also Oppression – those who speak out (p. 182)

St Peter & St Paul (29 June)

As we celebrate the Feast of St Peter and St Paul, we give thanks
for the life of the Church, built on their teaching and apostolic
ministry. We pray that the whole Church would be brought to
the unity for which they worked, and that all Christians would be
bold in the proclamation of the gospel.

Eternal God,
who chose your apostles Peter and Paul to spread the gospel to
    all the nations,
encourage us by their examples of faith and commitment,
inspire us through their writings
and help us to be true to you
in our calling to build up the Church in our own day,
through Jesus Christ our Lord.

For St Peter see also The companionship of God – trust in God (p. 102)

St Thomas the Apostle – truth through questioning (3 July)

Lord, we pray for your Church. As we recall Thomas'
questioning, which led to greater revelation, so we pray that, with
thoughtfulness, we would seek to explore the mystery of our faith
and long to be ever more deeply grounded in the truth.

Lord our God,
you sent your Son Jesus Christ to show your love to the world,
and through the work and weaknesses of the disciples
you revealed to us the magnitude of its glory.
Give us, we pray, like them,
hearts that yearn for the truth,
that seeking you with honesty and longing
we may find in this life some glimpse of your majesty,
and in the life to come, the full knowledge of your presence,
through the same Jesus Christ our Lord.

*See also Open-mindedness – help us to see the complexity of life
(p. 295)*

St Mary Magdalen (22 July)

Lord we pray for your Church. As we give thanks for Mary
Magdalen, witness to the risen Christ, so we pray that we may
bear faithful witness to Christ our Lord in the world.

God of love,
whose servant Mary Magdalen
came to know the risen Christ when he called her by name,
open our eyes to his risen presence with us day by day,
that we may find in him
our true identity and our fullest life,
through the same Jesus Christ our Lord.

See also The sick (p. 255)

St James the Great (25 July)

Lord God, as James the apostle left behind his nets to follow
Christ, learned the glory of his Lord in the transfiguration and
discovered the meaning of servant-leadership through Jesus'
teaching, so inspire us by his example and strengthen us by his
prayers, that we may follow Christ in devotion and service every
day of our lives.

Lord of love,
whose Son taught us that true greatness lies in being the servant of
    others,
help us, with James, to hear your call,
that, leaving behind all that keeps us far from you,
we may walk the path of discipleship,
knowing your glory
and serving your world,
through the same Jesus Christ our Lord.

See also Service – doers not merely hearers (p. 125)
and Civility – speak with kindness (p. 287)

Anne & Joachim (26 July, or St Joseph or Our Lady)

Lord, we pray for your world. As we remember Anne and
Joachim, so we pray for all parents: for all first-time parents, that
they would be calmed in their anxieties and strengthened in their
love; for all health professionals who support parents; and for any
who find parenthood a particular struggle or difficult to reconcile
with their own flourishing.

God, whose Son was content to be born into the life of a
    human family,
grant to all parents the love shown by Anne, Joachim, Mary
    and Joseph,
that through their care their children would grow in stature
    and maturity,
through their love their children would grow in confidence and in
    achievement,
and through their wisdom
they would find time as parents to care for themselves and their
    own relationships,
that all would be enabled to find joy in life
and discover their place as part of your all-embracing family,
in Jesus Christ our Lord.

William Wilberforce, Olaudah Equiano & Thomas Clarkson (30 July)

See Oppression – those who work to combat oppression (p. 187)
and Oppression – modern slavery and forced labour (p. 188)

The Transfiguration (6 August)

Lord, we pray for your Church. On this day when we celebrate
the Transfiguration of our Lord, we pray that, filled with his light,
we may know his glory and share his truth with our world.

God of gods,
whose Son was transfigured on the holy mountain,
that his disciples would know that he was God indeed,
open our eyes to his glory,
that through loving him we may grow more deeply in
    knowledge of you
and through serving him may reflect his radiance in our world,
through the same Jesus Christ our Lord.

St Dominic (8 August)

See Preachers (p. 89)
and Local community – city life (p. 202)

St Bartholomew – devotion to prayer (24 August)

Lord, as we thank you for the witness of Bartholomew
the apostle, may we devote ourselves to your service in the
communion of the Church he loved.

Lord God,
whose servant Bartholomew was nourished by the teaching of
    your Son
and shared in the common life of the apostles in devotion
    to prayer,
stir up within us the longing to pray,
that our days may be enfolded in your contemplation,
our decisions directed by your guidance
and our relationships deepened by your love,
through the same Jesus Christ our Lord.

St Augustine of Hippo (28 August)

Lord, on this day when the Church remembers St Augustine of
Hippo, teacher of the faith, we pray for your Church, that we
may come to know you as one who is closer to us than we are
even to ourselves.

God of our journey,
you have made us for yourself
and our hearts are restless until they find their rest in you.
Lead us on in the pilgrimage of life
and in the quest after truth,
that at the end of all our studies,
of all our philosophy,
and of all our striving after happiness and fullness of life,
we may come to know you in your divine simplicity
and ourselves as creatures fashioned for the enjoyment of
    your love,
in Jesus Christ our Lord.

St Gregory the Great (3 September)

Lord, we pray for your Church, that you would hear the prayers
of your servants and, by blessing our worship, help us, like St
Gregory, to draw near to you in the beauty of praise and in
service of the world.

God of beauty,
whose splendour fills the heavens
and whose creation is rich with reflections of your love,
pour on us and all who sing your praise
such eyes as may know true beauty,
such ears as may discern wise counsel
and such hearts as may love pure actions,
that enabled by your Spirit
we may know your will,
and, inflamed by your grace,
may show your glory to the world,
through Jesus Christ our Lord.

Part 1 The Church Year

Holy Cross Day (*14 September*)

Lord, as we find hope and glory in the mystery of the Cross, so
may we find in the struggles and difficulties of this life the comfort
of your presence and the truth of your purposes.

Lord Jesus Christ,
who endured the death of the Cross that we might live,
and who, under the weight of suffering,
revealed to us the true meaning of love, life and sacrifice,
strengthen us by the power of your victory over death,
that looking on the sign of the Cross
we may find our pain transformed into love,
our pride overwhelmed by humility
and our selfishness changed into service,
for you live and reign with the Father and the Holy Spirit,
one God, now and for ever.

St Matthew (*21 September*)

Lord, we pray for your Church. As we thank you for the witness
and writings of St Matthew, who found the truth of Christ in the
Hebrew Scriptures he loved, inspire us with his zeal to search the
Scriptures in study and to proclaim their truth in word and deed.

God of the ages,
whose servant Matthew saw in the coming of Christ
the realization of ancient prophecy and the fulfilment of holy law,
grant to us, who are nourished by his teaching,
the insight to know in our world the working of your
    eternal purposes
and the longing to bring your love to those in need of
    your healing,
through the same Jesus Christ our Lord.

St Michael & All Angels – angelic worship (29 September)

Lord, we pray for your Church, that strengthened by the whole host of angels we would be led into greater confidence in faith and greater devotion in worship.

Lord of hosts,
before whom Saints and Angels worship in the glory of the light
  of eternity,
bless our worship here on earth,
that in the beauty of music,
the wisdom of Scripture,
the power of sacrament
and the intimacy of silence,
our hearts may be raised to join the heavenly chorus
and find there the refreshment, inspiration and hope
to fill all the moments of our daily lives,
through Jesus Christ our Lord.

St Michael & All Angels – the Holy Guardian Angels (29 September)

Lord God, we pray for your world, that your holy angels would watch over all those who are vulnerable or in particular need this day, that through their ministry all people would come to know security and peace.

God of might,
whose servants the angels guide our paths and watch over our steps,
grant their strength to all those in most need of your aid.
By their ministry
protect the young,
heal the sick,
guide the perplexed,
bring home the lost
and, in their last hour,
draw the dying to yourself in peace,
through the power of one who himself knew our weaknesses,
even Jesus Christ our Lord.

St Luke (18 October)

Lord, as we celebrate St Luke's feast day, so we give thanks for his witness as an Evangelist to the truth of Christ, and pray that, together with the whole Church, we like him would be renewed in our love for all those at the margins of society.

Almighty God,
whose servant Luke saw you at work in those whom
    society ignores,
and recognized that greater love is often seen in those
    society condemns,
we pray that you would give us his compassion
to keep us from all self-satisfaction and pride,
and to make us keen seekers after your action in our world
and good pupils of those whose struggles in life
have taught them more deeply the meaning of your love,
through Jesus Christ our Lord.

See also Medicine – all those who work in medicine (p. 268)

St Simon & St Jude (28 October)

Lord, we pray for your Church. As we give thanks for your apostles Simon and Jude, we pray for all who seek to follow you today, and remembering especially Jude's patronage for all in desperate situations, we pray for all those struggling in their faith.

Lord God,
whose servants Simon and Jude served you with faithfulness in
    life and in death,
bless all those who are struggling to follow in your way this day.
Strengthen those whose faith is weak,
direct those who are in perplexity
and bring hope to those who are in despair,
that strengthened by the example of the two apostles
and aided by their prayers,
they may come to know once again the fullness of life
that is your will for us all in Jesus Christ our Lord.

All Saints' Day – the glorious variety of the saints (1 November)

Lord God, as we celebrate the gift of the Saints to encourage us
with their examples and to strengthen us by their prayers, so
we pray for your Church, that we may continue in their path of
faithfulness all our days.

God of all people,
we thank you that you have made us in a rich diversity,
so that each human being has something to offer to the tapestry
    of holiness.
As we honour those who in the brilliance of their variety have
    shown us your glory,
so we pray that our lives also may be bright with your Spirit,
revealing to the world that particular holiness for which you have
    created us,
in Jesus Christ our Lord.

All Saints' Day – teach us to be saints (1 November)

Lord, we pray for your Church on this All Saints' day, that
strengthened by the teaching of our forebears in the faith, we may
proclaim the gospel afresh in our generation.

Lord,
we thank you for the great calling you have put on each of
    our lives
and for the gift of your grace to enable us to fulfil all you
    would desire.
Teach us, we pray, how to be saints in this world.
When we feel worthless and hopeless, grant us your encouragement;
when we feel excited and glad, show us how to use our energy for
    your purposes;
and when we do not know which way to turn,
show us the path that leads us closer to you and to our own selves,
that inspired by the example of all those who have gone before us
we may truly be your holy people in our day,
ready to serve the needs of this broken and fragile world,
through Jesus Christ our Lord.

All Saints' Day – the virtues of the Saints (1 November)

Lord, as we give thanks for the communion of Saints, so we pray
for all your holy people at work in the world in our own day.

Lord of all,
through whose Saints we learn
the courage that is founded on faith,
the service that is founded on love
and the insight that is founded on hope,
grant us strength in our Christian discipleship,
that inspired by the lives of all the Saints and aided by their prayers,
we may become holy as you have called each one of us to be holy,
and the world may be led into the ways of justice and peace,
through Jesus Christ our Lord.

All Saints' Day – treasuring the inheritance of faith (1 November)

Lord, as in this season we celebrate all those Saints who have
gone before us, so we pray that in our own day we would preserve
the flame of faith, and in the power of your Spirit bring its light to
the whole world.

God of Abraham and Sarah,
God of Peter and Mary Magdalene,
God of the fathers and mothers of our faith,
you are with us always, to the end of time.
Help us in our own lives to walk in the way of your Son
by treasuring the inheritance of faith our ancestors have taught us,
that we would bring your love to our world
and all your people would be enabled to rejoice in freedom,
    peace and justice,
through Jesus Christ our Lord.

See also Unity – in all places of conflict (p. 151)

All Souls' Day (2 November)

Today we pray especially for all those who have died, whose lives have inspired us in our commitment to Christ and to one another, and for any whose loss is particularly on our hearts at this time.

Loving God,
by whom we were made
and in whom rests our hope of eternity,
gather into your gentle embrace
all those we love who have died,
that they may know the fullness of life with you
in that place where sorrow and sighing,
grief and pain are no more,
through Jesus Christ our Lord.

See also Mourners – keep them from despair (p. 238)

Guy Fawkes Night (5 November)

Lord, we pray for your world. As people in our country mark Guy Fawkes Night, so we pray for our national life, for harmony between people of different religion and politics, for an end to violence of word and deed and for a renewed commitment to working together towards a future of peace and justice for all.

God of all,
you created us to be one,
sharing our resources and talents for the good of all.
In your mercy, overcome the many barriers we put
    between ourselves
and the prejudices that keep us apart,
that inspired by your generous love
we may seek your will for our land
in a spirit of understanding, tolerance and mutual encouragement,
through Jesus Christ our Lord.

See also Local community – unity (p. 200)

Armistice Day – St Martin of Tours (11 November)

On this day we remember St Martin of Tours, a soldier who turned his life to the service of those in need. We pray for all those caught up in the conflicts of our world: for those who serve in the military and especially for those forced to serve against their will or under age, and for all those civilians caught up in the violence of war and civil strife. We pray too for all veterans of conflict and for any whose minds and bodies have been wounded by what they have experienced, and we pray for all charities that help to support and rehabilitate them. We pray for all those who have died in war and for all who mourn them. And we pray for the future of the world, that it may be one of peace and justice.

God of all nations,
whose Son showed your love
even amidst the violence of his brutal death,
pour out your peace upon our troubled world.
Bring to an end all armed conflict,
heal those wounded in strife,
and receive into your eternal kingdom
all those whose lives have been lost in war,
through Jesus Christ our Lord.

Remembrance Sunday – remembrance and commitment

Lord, we pray for your Church. As we mark Remembrance
Sunday throughout our land, we pray that our remembrance
would lead to a deeper respect for those who lost their lives in
war, and a greater commitment to working towards a better
future.

God of all,
you created us from nothing
and you know each one of us by name.
Grant us your love for each human life that passes through
    this world.
As a nation remembers,
help us to honour the dead,
to care for those whose lives are marked by the trauma of war
and to dedicate our lives to the service of peace,
that the sacrifice of those men and women who laid down
    their lives
may bear fruit in a future rich with peace, hope and joy,
through Jesus Christ our Lord.

Remembrance Sunday – those who fought for freedom

Lord, we pray for your world. We give thanks for the courage and
sacrifice of so many who by their actions bought our freedom. We
pray for those of them who have died, that they may rest in peace,
and for those still alive, that they may have a dignified old age and
know our gratitude to and our care for them.

Lord of love,
we thank you for the strength you give human beings
to serve others even at the cost of their own lives,
and we bless you especially today
for all who fought for the cause of freedom in armed conflict.
Give rest to the departed,
comfort to the living
and hope to us all,
that inspired by their example and their dedication
we may fight for continued peace
with the same tenacity and courage they showed in war,
through the same Jesus Christ our Lord.

Remembrance Sunday – the Church's ministry of reconciliation

On this Remembrance Sunday we pray particularly for the
Church's ministry to all those who have been injured in warfare,
both military personnel and civilians, and for the Church's
ministry of peace and reconciliation in our troubled world.

Lord God,
who created us to live in fellowship and unity with all the peoples
   of the earth,
grant your grace to all who serve you in the Church,
that we may be a blessing to our communities;
and renew our common life,
that we may be a witness to the world
of that peace and reconciliation
that come from knowing ourselves as part of one family
in Jesus Christ our Lord.

See also Ministry to military and in wartime (p. 89)
and War – for all its victims (p. 225)

St Andrew (30 November)

Lord, bless your Church, that inspired by the example of your
Apostle St Andrew, and aided by his prayers, we may serve you
in spreading the good news of Christ, and showing his love to
our world.

Almighty God,
whose Son called Andrew from his nets to serve the cause of
   the Gospel,
bless us in our ministry to the world,
that amidst the storms and tempests of human life
the Church would offer a true haven to those who struggle
and a safe refuge to all who are in distress,
through the same Jesus Christ our Lord.

St Stephen (26 December)

Lord, as we thank you for the example of St Stephen, deacon and
first martyr of the Church, so we pray for our Church life today,
that we would be strengthened to witness to the faith in all that
we do.

Lord God,
whose servant Stephen had the courage to face death in hope,
and the compassion to pray for the forgiveness of his murderers,
grant us, we pray, some share in his gifts,
that we may bring the truth of the gospel to the world
with boldness of word and with gentleness of deed,
through Jesus Christ our Lord.

See also Equality – overcoming hatred and division (p. 292)

St John, Apostle & Evangelist (27 December)

Lord, on this day when we give thanks for the witness and the
writings of St John, Apostle and Evangelist, we pray for your
Church, that like him we may spread the good news of your Son's
birth to the waiting world.

Lord God,
in the Incarnation of your Son
the word of life, which was from the beginning,
is made visible to human eyes,
audible to human ears
and tangible to human hands.
By his fellowship with us,
so strengthen us in all that we do,
that through our words and through our lives
your love would be made manifest again to the world,
and all peoples would live together in fellowship with you,
that our joy would be complete in Jesus Christ our Lord.

See also Hope – the light that darkness will never overcome (p. 294)

Holy Innocents (28 December)

Lord, we pray on this Holy Innocents' Day for the Church's
ministry to all those who suffer violence, asking for your
assistance in our own repentance for the unjust structures of our
past, and praying for our transformation into a fellowship more
reflective of your love and justice.

God of all,
whose Son Jesus Christ showed us the path of gentleness
and the demands of justice,
and who has called us to continue his work in the world,
be with us as we seek to witness to your truth,
that through commitment to your purposes,
courage in standing up for what is right
and compassion in serving those wounded by others,
we would be known as people of healing, reconciliation and peace,
through the same Jesus Christ our Lord.

The Martyrdom of St Thomas of Canterbury
(29 December)

Lord God, whose servant Thomas of Canterbury accepted death
in defence of the Church he loved, be with all those who seek to
follow you with integrity this day, that guided by your wisdom
and encouraged by your strength, we may run the race you have
set before us with perseverance and hope.

Loving God,
whose follower Thomas of Canterbury served you in his death
by holding fast to his faith to the end,
grant to us some share of his integrity,
that we may discern with wisdom,
speak with honesty
and live with confidence in the hope of eternal life,
through Jesus Christ our Lord.

PART 2

Prayers for the Life of the Church

The Universal Church

The Persecuted Church

The persecuted Church – give comfort, wisdom and courage (martyrs)

Lord we pray for your Church. [As we commemorate the martyr N,] we pray for all those who practise the faith in danger of their lives this day, that we may offer them the support of prayer and practical assistance.

Loving God,
whose Son, Jesus Christ, was true to your love
even to death on the Cross,
be with all Christians who live in places
where the preaching of the gospel risks persecution and death.
Give them comfort in their faith,
wisdom in their actions
and courage in all that they do,
through the same Jesus Christ our Lord.

The persecuted Church – God's guidance for the persecuted (martyrs)

We pray for all those who face persecution for their faith this day,
that they would be granted wisdom, courage and hope.

God of all,
in whose hand is the sun's rising and its setting,
the dawning of the day and the lengthening of the shadows,
be with all those whose trust in you
leads them towards the darkness of suffering and death this day.
In all their dangers be their protector,
in all their fears be their comforter,
in all their perplexity be their discernment,
that having faith in you, they may find in the power of your Spirit
the ability to live in the light, even in the darkness of this
    world's violence,
and the ability to go on loving, even when surrounded by so
    much hate,
after the pattern of your only Son,
Jesus Christ our Lord.

The persecuted Church (St George) – be their shield

Lord, on this day when we remember St George, the soldier who
offered his life for the faith, so we pray for your whole Church, and
especially for those who are persecuted for their hope in Christ this
day, that we may support them with prayer and practical action.

Heavenly Father,
you long for each of us to flourish in faith and grow in love,
and yet so often jealousy of another's contentment leads us
    to cruelty.
Be with all those this day
whose belief in Christ and whose devotion to the Church
brings them into danger of violence, imprisonment,
    discrimination or even death,
that knowing you as their shield of protection and their comfort
    in times of trouble,
they may continue to follow faithfully the path laid before them
    by your Son,
Jesus Christ our Lord.

Part 2 Prayers for the Life of the Church

The Unity of the Church

Unity of the Church in diversity

Lord of all life, we pray for your Church, that through this
wonderful and great mystery you would teach us, strengthen us
and nurture us.

Lord God,
you have called all people to yourself,
and your love will not let your children keep apart from others.
Help us to experience, we pray, in the rich diversity of
    our backgrounds,
the unity we share as children of the same heavenly Father,
and help us to treasure our particularity,
knowing that each one of us has something unique to show to
    the world
of your wisdom and your care,
in Jesus Christ our Lord.

Unity of the Church – brothers and sisters

Lord, we pray that your Church may be a true home for all the
peoples of the earth.

O Lord, you have called us into one body
to worship you in spirit and in truth.
Grant us your grace to live together
as brothers and sisters in Christ.
Take from us all hostility and lack of understanding,
that we may bear witness to the world
to that generous love you have revealed to us
in Jesus Christ our Lord.

Unity of the Church – as the Father and the Son are one

Lord, we pray for your Church, that we may grow together in
unity, in understanding and in confidence.

O God whose life is love,
your Son taught us that we should be one, just as you and he
    are one.
Inspire your Church with the gift of unity, we pray,
that leaving behind all pride and hardness of heart,
and reaching out to one another in openness and humility,
we would come to experience for ourselves
the joy of dwelling together in harmony
and the delight of learning from the wisdom of one another,
in Jesus Christ our Lord.

Unity of the Church – learning from one another

Lord God, we pray for your Church, that we may grow together
into ever greater unity in love.

Lord Jesus Christ,
you taught your disciples to be one,
even as you and the Father are one,
and you call us in our own day to work for that unity which is
    your gift and will.
Send your Spirit of concord into the hearts of all Christian people,
that we may have the humility to learn the truth that others bring,
the wisdom to find words that give voice to a shared and greater
    vision of God,
and the love that refuses to rest until all are reconciled as one
    family of faith in you,
O Jesus Christ our Lord.

Week of Prayer for Christian Unity

Unity of the Church – week of prayer for Christian Unity

Lord, we pray for your Church. [In this week of prayer for Christian Unity] we pray that all Christians may grow closer to one another in faith, in understanding and in love.

God our Creator,
you have made us to find joy in fellowship
and to find learning in attending to the wisdom of others.
Strengthen all Christians by the Holy Spirit,
that we may live together in your love and your peace.
Give us, we pray, your gifts of understanding, patience
    and openness,
that we may grow together ever more visibly,
as the one Church worshipping you, the one true God,
through your Son, Jesus Christ our Lord.

Unity of the Church – week of prayer for Christian Unity – church leaders

Lord, we pray for your Church, that strengthened by your power we would have the courage to preach your word to a waiting world. In this week of prayer for Christian unity, we pray for deeper relationships between all Christian denominations, and particularly for our leaders, that they would guide us in the ways that lead to unity.

God of gods,
hope of the nations
and light beyond all light,
direct the paths of all those who lead us,
that as gentle pastors,
as faithful teachers
and as brave prophets,
they may enable us to work towards the unity
that is your gift and will,
in Jesus Christ our Lord.

Unity of the Church – week of prayer for Christian Unity – theologians

Lord, we pray for your Church, that in this week of prayer
for Christian Unity you would send your Holy Spirit on us
afresh to bring us into that unity for which you long. We pray
especially today for the work of theologians, who seek to deepen
understanding between different traditions, and for all involved in
inter-denominational dialogue.

God our redeemer,
in your Son Jesus Christ there is no Jew or Greek,
no slave or free,
no male or female.
Grant us, we pray, your vision of the world,
that we would be led from the smallness of our comfortable pride
    and self-righteousness,
to the challenge of your expansive truth,
through the same Jesus Christ our Lord.

Unity of the Church – week of prayer for Christian Unity – practical cooperation

Lord, we pray for your Church. In this week of prayer for
Christian Unity, we pray for deeper understanding and love
between Christians of all traditions, praying especially today for
all those Christians who work together in the service of the needs
of others in charities, foodbanks, schools and nursing homes.

God,
whose unity is lived out in the joy of the eternal Trinity,
be with all those who seek to follow you through your Son,
that we would look beyond our own traditions and habits of mind
to see you at work in the lives and worship of others,
that through knowing and loving them
we may come to see more of the greatness of your truth,
through the same Jesus Christ our Lord.

See also Unity – finding joy in diversity (p. 157)

Unity of the Church – the Anglican Communion

Lord God, as we thank you for the gift of our Anglican
Communion, we pray that through faithfulness to our vocation
we may bring your love to our world.

God of all truth,
we give you thanks for our Anglican Communion,
for the particular gifts and graces that you have bestowed on it
and for our commitment to sharing what we have received
with other Christians of all traditions
for the upbuilding of your kingdom.
In your mercy, lead us in your way,
that we would know the truth
and be set free to serve you in worship, in action and in love,
through Jesus Christ our Lord.

The Local Church

A Diocese

God our Father, we pray for the life of our diocese, that enriched
by your grace we may witness to your eternal truth in our own
time and place.

God of us all,
you have poured on us a rich diversity of gifts
and call us to offer all you have given us to your service and to
    one another.
Bless all those who minister in this diocese,
that in the beauty of worship,
the resourcing of ministry
and the work of education,
human lives would be transformed
and your love and truth would be known by ever more people,
through Jesus Christ our Lord.

A Cathedral Church

Lord, we pray for your Church and for this sacred place, and our
mission of bringing people together in the love and peace of Christ.

Heavenly Father, whose love knows no boundaries
and who has called us together in worship this day,
grant that this house of prayer may be a true home for all nations,
a focus of prayer, learning and hospitality for this diocese
and a place of sanctuary and peace for all who need your restoration
from the sufferings and disappointments of this world,
for the sake of your Son, Jesus Christ our Lord.

A Church Building

A church building – bless this house of prayer

God of all, we thank you for the gift of this sacred place, that here
we may know your presence and be inspired in your service.

Almighty God,
the heaven of heavens cannot contain you,
yet you have promised to be present
wherever two or three are gathered together in your name.
Grant, we pray, your heavenly blessing to this house of prayer,
which has been built for your honour and glory;
and sanctify with your abiding presence
the lives of all those who you draw to this place,
this day and always,
through Jesus Christ our Lord.

A church building and its congregation

Holy God, we pray for this church, that all those who are drawn
to this place may be strengthened in faith, hope and love.

Lord God,
we thank you for the gift of this holy place,
set apart by the devotion of generations
to be a house of prayer for all people.
Be with all those who are with us at this time,
that they may come to know more deeply the love you have
    for them,
the call for which you fashioned them before their birth,
and your vision of a creation renewed by your infinite grace,
through Jesus Christ our Lord.

A church building – an inspiring gift from previous generations

Lord, we pray for your Church, that, treasuring our rich
inheritance, we would be inspired to witness in our own day to all
that we have received from our forebears in the faith.

Creator God,
we thank you for the glory of all you have made,
and for the skill that has led people through all the centuries
to fashion things of beauty, as songs of praise in stone.
As we give you thanks for the inspiration that
countless pilgrims and visitors have found in this church,
open our eyes again, we pray,
that renewed in our own wonder for all that is around us,
we may praise you in worship, in speaking words of gentleness
    and in deeds of love,
through Jesus Christ our Lord.

A church building and its power to inspire mission

Lord of glory, as we give thanks for the beauty of this place, may
it inspire us to share our vision of your beauty and goodness
with others.

Lord our God,
we thank you for the gift of this house of prayer,
for the beauty of its construction,
for the glory of the worship that takes place within it
and for the fellowship of the community that lives and works
    around it.
May our life here inspire us to reach out to the world,
with words of joy, hope and peace in troubled times,
and may the depth of our hospitality
enrich the lives of all those who enter these walls,
through Jesus Christ our Lord.

A church building and its inspiration to artists
(an arts festival)

Lord God, we thank you for the inspiration that you have given
your Church; for the faithfulness of those who have built and
maintained this church over the centuries and who have taken
part in its common life of prayer. And we pray particularly today
for our ministry to this [city] and our role in sustaining and
encouraging the artistic life of this place.

Lord, you have given human beings a sense of the sublime,
that through art and music and writings
our lives may be enriched
and our hearts may be led to your eternal beauty.
Strengthen us in this place,
that through our stewardship of our buildings,
our ministry of hospitality and our daily work,
this place may continue to inspire artists
and be evermore enriched by their creativity,
through Jesus Christ our Lord.

Our Welcome

Our welcome (Mothering Sunday)

Lord, we pray for your Church. [On this day when we remember the Church as our mother,] we pray that nourished by the Church's care, and instructed by her teaching, we may welcome many into this place, to be inheritors of that heavenly Jerusalem which is the mother to us all.

God our Creator,
you call us together to share in the community of the Church,
that through our love for one another the world may come
    to believe.
Grant us the wisdom to be open to others,
the sensitivity to learn from their insights
and the commitment to welcome them in and show them kindness
    and care,
that through our wonderful diversity
we would glimpse something of the greatness of your truth,
in Jesus Christ our Lord.

The ministry of welcome

Heavenly Father, we pray for your Church, that we may be generous in our welcome to all people and open to being transformed in your love.

Lord God,
you called us to find friendship with one another in your Church
and together to serve our world.
Bless our fellowship with your Spirit,
that we may be strengthened through the example and the
    encouragement of others
and open our eyes once again to the needs of this world,
that through prayer, hospitality and works of practical service
we may bring your love to all those who need it most,
through Jesus Christ our Lord.

Our Worship

Our worship – be with us as we worship

Lord God, we pray for the Church that is animated by your
Holy Spirit.

Heavenly Father,
by whose grace the whole of humanity is called to praise you,
bless the worship of this place,
be with us in all our singing and our speaking
and in the meditations of our hearts,
that as we adore you in the beauty of holiness,
so our lives may be transformed by your Spirit
to reflect the pattern of that life of self-giving love,
known to us in your Son, Jesus Christ our Lord.

Our worship – a hymn of praise throughout the world

Lord, we pray for your Church that, renewed by the power of
your Spirit, we may serve you in worship, in service and in love.

God of all creation,
all things were made by you and by your will they are held in being.
Strengthen those who call on your name,
that in harmony with our sisters and brothers throughout
   the world,
and with the whole of the created order,
we may sing to you a hymn of praise
and live lives full of righteousness, gentleness and joy,
through Jesus Christ our Lord.

Our worship – free us from distractions

Lord, we pray for your Church, that through our prayer and our work the whole world would resound with your praise.

Heavenly Father,
your love is made known in the gift of life
and your glory is expressed in the beauty of all you have made.
Take from our hearts all distraction and anxiety,
that in peace we may offer to you our hymn of praise
and our song of thanksgiving,
in union with the whole created order and all the hosts of heaven,
through Jesus Christ our Lord.

Our worship – inspiration for service

Lord, we pray for your Church, that in our worship you would be praised in spirit and in truth.

God of glory,
source of our being
and worthy of our praise,
receive, we pray, the prayers of those who gather in worship
    this day,
that we may come to know you in stillness,
come to serve you in our actions
and come to love you as our hearts rise up to you in song and
    in speech,
through Jesus Christ our Lord.

Our worship – be with us in our worship

Lord, we pray for your Church, that we may come before your presence together in the unity of sacred silence and worship.

Lord, whose coming is with might
but whose will is for peace,
whose glory fills the earth
but whose longing is for each human soul,
be with us in our worship and in our lives,
that we may know in this life your guidance and your care
and that at the last we may be brought
to that moment which goes beyond the perfection of music
    and silence
in the pure contemplation of your presence,
through Jesus Christ our Lord.

Our worship – a foretaste of heaven

Lord, we pray for your Church, that knowing the promises of
eternal life we may come to a foretaste of heaven in our worship
and in lives of love.

God of eternity,
whose glory is our destiny
and whose peace is our lasting home,
stir up our hearts in praise,
that as we sing of your majesty we may know heaven's joy,
and as we attend to your silence we may know heaven's calm,
through him in whose life God and humanity are one,
even Jesus Christ our Lord.

Our worship – servers and musicians

Heavenly Father,
in worship you give us the privilege to participate on earth in the
    life of heaven.
Strengthen with creativity, skill and faithfulness
all those who serve in the sanctuary,
all those who sing in the choir
and all those through whose talents
we see more of your perfect beauty,
revealed to us in the face of Jesus Christ our Lord.

Church Music

Church music as part of our ministry

Lord, as we thank you for the gift of music, we pray that our
whole lives would be tuned to your service.

Lord God,
through your Spirit you inspire us to praise you
and through your gifts you give us the ability to sing your praise.
Strengthen and renew the work of our churches,
that in the harmony of music,
the beauty of worship,
the generosity of welcome
and the service of those in need,
we would do your will and bring others to know your truth,
through Jesus Christ our Lord.

Church music – join in the angelic chorus

Lord, we pray for your Church, that filled with the sound of your
praise we may show the world the joy of loving and serving you.

O God and King,
you are worshipped by saints and angels in the eternal joy
    of heaven.
Receive our songs of praise,
that as we join our voices with their chorus
we would be filled with thankfulness for your gift of music,
renewed in our own creativity
and inspired to serve you,
by bringing your love and your joy to all the corners of the world,
through Jesus Christ our Lord.

Church music – deepening our worship

Lord, we thank you for the gift of music to enliven our worship
and to raise our hearts, and pray for those who offer their musical
talents in your service, that through their singing and playing they
would develop their skill and increase their fulfilment.

God our Creator,
who fashioned the world in the beginning
and grants each of us gifts to give you praise,
we thank you for the precious treasure of music,
for its power to move and inspire us
and for its ability to deepen our worship of you.
Sustain all those who offer their skills to your service,
that through their work
many would hear the echo of your love
and come to know the beauty of your being,
through Jesus Christ our Lord.

Church music – an image of the harmony of the world

Lord, we thank you for the gift of music to inspire us in worship
and for the gift of one another to encourage us in faith.

Creator God,
in the beginning you fashioned a universe in harmony,
and yet so often we choose the path of discord;
you created us to sing of your glory,
and yet so often we fail to join the world's hymn of your praise.
Stir up within us that inspiration that you have planted in each of
    our hearts,
that raising our voices together,
the whole world would resound in gladness
and all our worship would be joined with the angels' eternal song,
through Jesus Christ our Lord.

Church music – song deeper than words

Heavenly Father, whose glory is greater than our words can
express, help us through our music to raise our hearts to you in
worship and to open our souls to your love.

Almighty God,
we thank you for all the gifts you have given us,
and especially today for the gift of song
to express that which goes deeper in the human spirit than any
     words can name.
Help us, through our singing and through our listening,
to be attuned to the action of your Spirit in our hearts
and to sense what eye has not seen and ear has not heard,
those things that you have prepared for all who love you,
through Jesus Christ our Lord.

Church Musicians

Church musicians – all church musicians

Lord, we pray for your Church, that in the joy of the Resurrection
our lives would be transformed and our hopes renewed in Christ.
On this day we give special thanks for the gift of music and for all
those who offer their talents and inspiration to the glory of God.

Creator of all,
you made our universe to be full of order and harmony
and you call us to join our voices to the songs of heaven.
Bless, we pray, all those who create beauty in music,
that through their passion and skill
they may bring us on this earth to hear the echoes of the
     angels' song
and to be caught up in the mystery of their eternal worship of the
     one true God,
Father, Son and Holy Spirit.

Church musicians – the musicians of this church

Generous God, we thank you for all those who offer their musical
talents in your service, and pray that they would be inspired with
your gifts of skill, dedication and joy in their work.

O God,
who gave to human beings the gift to make music
and the desire to turn this skill to the service of your praise,
we thank you for all those who make music in this place;
for their dedication and ability in their craft
and for the inspiration they bring to each one of us.
Grant that, through your Holy Spirit,
and by the glory of their song,
we may glimpse something of your perfect beauty
and aspire to harmony and goodness in our own lives,
through Jesus Christ our Lord.

A Church Choir

A church choir – grant them skill, joy and understanding

Lord, we pray for our choir, that as they sing in your worship,
they may be filled with your peace and your joy.

Creator God,
who formed the world from nothing
to be a place of beauty to all those who look on it,
we thank you for all the creative gifts that you have given us.
Grant, we pray, to those who sing in this place an ever growing
    skill in music,
a joyful heart in their work,
and a deepening understanding of the God whom we gather
    to worship,
through Jesus Christ our Lord.

A church choir – an echo of the angels' song

Lord, we pray for your Church, that all our worship, filled with
your Spirit, may give us a glimpse of your eternal beauty.

God of all,
whose wisdom fashioned all creation in harmony,
to make by its operation the music of your praise,
grant to all those who sing in this place
joy in their talents,
growth in their understanding
and fulfilment in their fellowship with one another,
that in their music we may hear on this earth
the echo of the angels' song of worship,
through Jesus Christ our Lord.

A church choir – departing choristers

Lord, we pray for your Church, that in the beauty of music and
the glory of worship we may know your majesty and your love;
and we pray especially for all those who have come to the end of
their time in our choir today.

Lord of glory,
who gave to your human creation the power to fashion things of
   beauty for your praise,
bless with your holy inspiration
all those who share in the talent of making music.
Guide them in their learning,
encourage them in their development
and rejoice with them in the delight and discipline of performance;
and this day, for our leavers,
help them to know the depth of our gratitude
and to feel for themselves the satisfaction of a job well done,
through Jesus Christ our Lord.

Bell Ringers

God of our joy, we pray for all those who make the music of bells,
that as we are called to prayer by their sound, so we may know
ourselves to be called to service by your love.

Lord God,
whose Church summons the faithful to worship by the music
   of bells,
so tune all our hearts by your love and your laws,
that we may serve you
in worship,
in proclamation,
in reconciliation
and in service of the poor,
through Jesus Christ our Lord.

Church People

Church Leaders

Church leaders

Lord our guide, bless those who lead your Church, that through their teaching and their care your flock may flourish in all its ways.

Lord of all life,
you never cease from calling people to turn and follow you,
and you empower us with your Spirit to do marvellous things in
  your service.
Strengthen all those who lead your Church in our day with your
  many gifts,
that they in turn may strengthen all your people in their ministry
to bring your light to a world so in need of your truth and
  your love,
through Jesus Christ our Lord.

Church leaders – their ministry

Lord God, strengthen all those whom you call to authority in the Church, that under their guidance we may know your truth and serve you in love.

God of all,
through your mercy you direct the ways of human hearts into the
    paths of justice and peace.
Grant to all those given authority in your Church
that they may minister your grace to those who seek after you
    in hope,
that they may preach your word to those who long for
    understanding of holy things
and that they may serve you faithfully in serving the poor and
    needy of this world,
through Jesus Christ our Lord.

The Ordained Ministry

Ordained ministry – those seeking ordination (Ember Days)

Lord, we pray for your Church, and on this Ember Day for all
those being ordained at this time, remembering especially all those
to be ordained in this diocese.

Almighty God,
you know us from before we were born
and have formed each one of us to fulfil some special calling in
    your service.
Be with all those whose journey leads them to seek ordination in
    your Church.
Invigorate them in their excitement,
calm them in their anxieties,
help them to know your presence with them at this time
    of transition
and be their constant guide, companion and friend
on the journey of life that lies ahead,
through Jesus Christ our Lord.

Ordained ministry – the ministry of bishops

Lord, we pray for the bishops of your Church, that strengthened
in their faith, they may build up your flock in wisdom and love.

God of our calling,
You fashion within us gifts, inspiration and character
to prepare us for the service of your kingdom.
Strengthen all those called to the ministry of a bishop throughout
    your Church, that by the guiding of your Holy Spirit
they may be gentle pastors, wise leaders
and faithful stewards of the mysteries they have received,
for the service of all God's people,
through Jesus Christ our Lord.

Ordained ministry – supporters and encouragers of the Church and her ministers (Ethelbert, King of Kent – 25 February)

Lord God, we pray for your Church. [On this day when we
remember Ethelbert, King of Kent, who received Augustine on his
mission from Rome and allowed him to set up the Church in this
land, so] we pray for all those who support the missionary activity
and pastoral life of the Church, whatever their beliefs.

God of all,
you have poured out on humanity a rich diversity of gifts,
that alongside preachers and missionaries
others would be called to share in their work
through support and hospitality,
through friendship and encouragement
and through protection and assistance.
Guide and direct all those who support the life of the Church
    this day,
that they would continue to offer wise advice, practical help
and, when needed, rebuke with loving hearts,
that drawing on all they provide,
we would be drawn into greater truth and serve with
    greater faithfulness,
through Jesus Christ our Lord.

Preachers

Preachers (St Dominic) – listening as well as speaking

Lord, we pray for your Church, that [as we give thanks this day
for St Dominic and the Order of Preachers which he founded,]
we would embrace our vocation to seek after truth and present it
with love to others.

O God,
you send us messengers in each generation
to preach the good news and to minister your love to our world.
Inspire us with your Holy Spirit,
that we may listen with attentiveness to the truth others bring
and have the confidence to speak of the knowledge we
    have received,
through Jesus Chris our Lord.

Ministry to the Military

Ministry to the military and in wartime – the suffering of war (Armistice Day)

Lord, we pray for your Church, that we may always offer
compassion and understanding to those in need. We pray
especially for the Church's ministry to our armed forces, giving
thanks for the work of all military chaplains and their assistants,
and praying for strength for them in all they do.

Lord God,
there is no place that is beyond your concern
and no depth of suffering and sadness beyond your love.
Be with your Church, we pray,
that we may offer the light of hope in places of despair,
the warmth of human company in places of loneliness
and the refreshment of peace in places of chaos and war,
through Jesus Christ our Lord.

Beginnings & Endings

A new ministry

On this day we pray especially for N, giving thanks for the call
of God that has brought him/her here, and praying that s/he
may find a life in this community that brings him/her fulfilment,
happiness and friendship.

God of our calling,
you lead us wisely through the journey of our lives,
ever revealing to us new possibilities of service
and new places to make our home.
Bless N in his/her new ministry as N,
that through his/her work with us,
the love, creativity and joy of Jesus Christ
would be more fully known in our community, [our city and
   county] and our world,
through the same Jesus Christ our Lord.

New ministries and initiatives

God of life, in whose Son there is a new creation, bless all that we
begin afresh today, that under your protection and through your
guidance it may bear plentiful fruit for ourselves and for others.

God our redeemer,
through your mercy you make all things new.
We pray for a renewed outpouring of your Spirit on all that is
   new within our Church:
on all those entering into new ministries,
on all those attempting new initiatives
and on all those discovering new depths of spirituality
   within themselves,
that strengthened by your power
and in the knowledge of your steadfastness,
Christians everywhere may have the confidence
to seek you in worship, to serve you in their lives and to speak of
   you to others,
through Jesus Christ our Lord.

Departure of a minister or member of the congregation

God of all time, as we give you thanks for the gift of N's time with us and his/her ministry in this place, we pray for your blessing on him/her as s/he takes the next step in his/her journey of life.

Lord of all,
we thank you that you call us in your service
in a rich and beautiful variety of ways.
As we give thanks for the ministry of our brother/sister N
    among us,
so may we be inspired by his/her wisdom and his/her faithfulness,
to walk this day and always in your way,
to seek out your will for our lives
and to grow together in your love,
as your pilgrim people on this earth,
through Jesus Christ our Lord.

Departure of a minister or member of the congregation – pilgrimage of life

Lord, who calls us each day to follow, bless your servant N as s/he prepares to leave us and begin the next chapter of his/her life, that in all s/he does, s/he would know your presence and your peace.

Lord God,
our beginning and our ending,
our companion on our journeys
and our homecoming at their ends,
be with N and all of us on our pilgrimage through life,
that through all our experiences on earth
we may come to know you more deeply
as our king and our friend,
in Jesus Christ our Lord.

THE CHRISTIAN LIFE

Prayer

Our Prayer Life

Prayer – commitment to prayer

Lord, we pray for your Church, for strength to set time apart for
prayer and for dedication in our worship and study.

Lord God,
you call us to follow you each day,
and the more we seek you, the more we find of your truth.
Stir up our spirits within us,
that renewed in our desire for you
and watchful in our prayer,
we may open up the space in our lives
where you may be found in stillness,
through Jesus Christ our Lord.

Prayer – contemplation

Lord of love, place within our hearts that longing for you, that
each day we may seek you in prayer, tell you of our needs and
listen for your voice.

Lord of all,
you are present to us in each moment
and make that presence known in the silence of prayer.
Help us to commit ourselves afresh to seeking you in contemplation,
help us to know your love in our moments of reflection
and help us, amid all the noise and busyness of the world,
to know your call on our lives and to follow it,
through Jesus Christ our Lord.

Prayer – honesty in prayer

Lord, we pray for all people, that, in confidence that you hear us,
we may persist in prayer today and always.

God of light and darkness,
our beginning and our end,
by your Spirit inspire us to raise our voices to you.
When we rejoice, may we tell you of our joy,
when we struggle and are in confusion, may we speak to you of
    our pain,
when our love for others puts their needs so profoundly before
    our eyes,
help us to form our prayer,
that we may find in our own lives, and in the lives of others,
the pattern and work of your Son,
our Saviour Jesus Christ.

Prayer – transformation through prayer

Lord, renew your Church, that our hearts would be transformed
by our worship and our world transformed by our service.

God of all,
your being is love
and your desire is for us to grow in relationship with you.
Bless us on our journey,
that as we glorify you in praise and seek you in stillness
we may come to know you as the end of all our striving
and come to experience you as our faithful companion on the way,
through Jesus Christ our Lord.

Prayer – watchful in prayer

Lord, we pray for your Church, that following the Lord's
command we may be watchful in prayer.

Lord, you gave us the gift and privilege of prayer
and are always calling us into deeper relationship with you.
Forgive us when our prayers are infrequent or half-hearted,
renew our zeal and our love for prayer
and help us to hear your voice in times of contemplation in the
    silence of our hearts,
that when your Son comes
we may not be found sleeping
but awake to your promises
and ready to greet him,
through the same Jesus Christ our Lord.

Prayer & Service

Prayer & service – prayer as the inspiration for service

Heavenly Father, as we call on you in prayer, teach us to serve
you in our lives.

Lord God,
your Son Jesus Christ came to make all things new.
Refresh us by the power of your Spirit,
that through the stillness of prayer
and the energy of service
we may discover afresh your call on our lives
and your unconditional love for our selves,
through Jesus Christ our Lord.

Prayer & service – to know and follow the example of Christ

Lord, we pray for your Church, that seeking you we may find you, and that in our longing for you we would find the purpose and fulfilment of our lives in your service.

God of all eternity,
who sent your Son into the world to bring us salvation,
show us your mercy,
that enlightened by his grace
we may live lives worthy of his example,
and in the silence discern the still voice of his call,
through the same Jesus Christ our Lord.

Times of Prayer

Prayer – a time of prayer, introduction to prayer

(based on the Cantique de Jean Racine)

Lord, we pray for your Church, that enlightened by the gospel and renewed in its hope we may serve you in generosity and love.

Eternal God,
as we break the stream of this day's activities to turn our prayer
    to you,
inspire us with the light of your love.
Set us free from the bonds of busyness and self-obsession
and help us to be transformed
by the powerful warmth of your love,
that we may share with those whom we meet
all those many gifts we have received at your hands,
through Jesus Christ our Lord.

Prayer – at morning

Prayer – at morning, direct us this day

Lord, as we thank you for the gift of this new day, we pray that you would bless us that in all our actions, our words and our thoughts we would make the hours that lie ahead an offering in your service.

God of the ages,
to whom one thousand years are like a single day,
we thank you for bringing us in safety to this morning.
Direct our steps and enlighten our hearts,
that in all things
we may act with your wisdom, your joy and your love,
through Jesus Christ our Lord.

Prayer – at morning, our daily bread

Lord, we pray for this day and for your presence with us on our journey through it. May you may bring us all we need to serve those we meet.

O God,
whose Son taught us to pray for our daily bread,
strengthen us for all the labours of this day.
When we are hungry, bring us your sustenance,
when we are tired, bring us your encouragement,
when we are uncertain, bring us your guidance,
that we may come to the setting of the sun
in thankfulness for all that has passed today,
and with enthusiasm, after rest,
to serve you once again tomorrow,
in Jesus Christ our Lord.

Prayer – at morning, learning each day

Lord, we pray for this day, that through it, in ways large and small, we would come to know more of the goodness of your creation, the plan you have for our lives and the love you bear for every human being.

Eternal God,
in your mercy you give us, each day,
the opportunity to turn our hearts more fully to you and to
    our world.
Direct our steps,
that we may not pass by unnoticed
the many opportunities for learning that these hours will bring.
Help us to recognize our vocation in moments of joy,
to expand our vision in meetings with others
and to recognize your love and your healing in moments of failure
    and hurt,
that we may see this day not only as a time that will pass
but as a step on the journey towards your unending love,
through Jesus Christ our Lord.

Prayer – at morning, those in need today

Lord, as we thank you for the blessings you have given us to enjoy today, we pray for all those who awaken with us to pain, sorrow, hunger or poverty this morning.

God of all peoples,
you know each one of us by name
and care for each one of us with a father's love.
As we thank you for all that lies ahead of us today,
we pray for all those for whom this morning brings pain.
Grant relief to those who suffer
and assistance to those in need,
that through your company and through the work of our
    whole society
they too may come to know mornings of joy once again,
through Jesus Christ our Lord.

Prayer – at evening

Prayer – at evening

Lord, we pray for your Church, that through our worship we may
experience on this earth the life of heaven.

Lord our God,
we thank you for the gift of this day
and we hallow it with our praises.
At this evening hour, hear our prayer
and gather up into one all our labours, our words and
    our feelings,
that, knowing all our cares to be held in your love,
we may find rest and peace
in your Son, Jesus Christ our Lord.

Prayer – at evening for a peaceful night

Lord, we pray for your Church, that you would show us the love
you have for us in each moment of our lives.

God of love,
you formed us before we were born
and promised us that wherever we go, we cannot be far from you.
Be close to us this night and fill us with your comfort,
that resting secure in your care and your delight
we may find rest and peace,
through Jesus Christ our Lord.

Prayer – at evening, God our rest and our restoration

Lord, we pray for your Church, that in your mercy you would
hear our prayer and bring us more deeply into your love.

O Lord, our refuge,
our hope and our peace,
be with us this night
as our protector and our salvation.
Calm our anxieties,
ease our fears
and banish our anger,
that we may find in you our true rest
and our perfect restoration,
through Jesus Christ our Lord.

The Companionship of God

The companionship of God – at all times

God our Father, we pray that you would be with us to guide and
to comfort at all the times of our life.

Lord almighty,
whose Son Jesus Christ knew the joys and sorrows of human life,
be with us in times of hope and in times of fear,
be with us in days of delight and in nights of sorrow,
be with us in new beginnings and in moments of ending,
that through all the turmoil of life
we may know you as our rock, our redeemer and our hope,
in Jesus Christ our Lord.

The companionship of God – in good times and in bad

Lord, we pray for your Church, that enlightened by the love of
Christ we would serve you in lives of gentleness and compassion.

God of all,
in whom we live and move and have our being,
be with us in all the moments of this fleeting life,
that awake or asleep,
in joy or in sorrow,
in exaltation or in pain
we may know the warmth of your company
and the delight of your love,
through Jesus Christ our Lord.

The companionship of God in the changing seasons of life

Eternal God, in whom there is no shadow of change, be with us, we pray, in all the changes of this life, bringing us hope and peace and joy.

Creator God,
source of our being
and our life's goal,
be with us through the changing seasons of life, we pray.
When all is joyful and encouraging,
give us the confidence and the gratefulness to rejoice,
when all seems hopeless and forlorn,
give us the strength of your presence and hope for the future,
that we may know our every moment to be lived with you,
in the endless life of your risen Son,
Jesus Christ our Lord.

The companionship of God – help us to find our happiness in you

Lord, we pray for your Church, that we may be filled with joy and thankfulness in our faith.

God our life and our love,
our companion and our goal,
help us to find in our faith in you
such joy as will make living a delight,
such thankfulness as will lead us to wonder
and such hope as will bring us to eternal peace,
through one who though rich became poor,
for the sake of his surpassing love,
even Jesus Christ our Lord.

The companionship of God – in times of difficulty

Loving God, we pray for your companionship in all times of
difficulty in our life, that by your guidance and your care we
might come to that fullness of life which is your will for us.

Almighty God,
who gave us your only Son to be the pioneer of salvation,
send the Holy Spirit, we pray, on all those who seek to follow in
 his path.
In times of doubt bring us hope,
in times of anxiety bring us peace,
in times of uncertainty bring us wisdom
and in times of loneliness bring us the joyful gift of your company,
for the sake of one who called his followers not servants but friends,
even Jesus Christ our Lord.

The companionship of God – trust in God (Peter walks on the waves)

Lord, we pray for your Church, that we may find the faith
to follow your Son, wherever he may lead us and however
impossible it may seem at first to make the journey.

O God of trust,
through love Peter desired to be with his Lord across the waves,
through faith he was enabled to walk on the face of the waters
and through the compassion of your Son he was sustained in his
 time of doubt and danger.
Grant to us all such love that we may seek your presence,
such faith that we may follow whatever path you set before us
and such trust that we may speak honestly to you,
knowing that our words, our actions and our very being
are sustained by your eternal care,
in Jesus Christ our Lord.

The companionship of God – his comfort

Lord, we pray for your Church, that we may pour out our needs
to you in prayer and know your comfort in all times of trial.

Lord our God,
you hear our cry
and you know our weeping.
In moments of lament bring us your hope,
wipe away our tears,
and out of the night of sorrow
bring the dawn of joy,
that all the trials and difficulties of this life
may lead us only to a closer relationship with you,
in Jesus Christ our Lord.

The companionship of God – we change but you are the same

Lord, we pray for your Church, that in good times and bad we
may find that contentment that comes from knowing you.

God our beginning and our end,
in whose perfect peace our lives are made whole,
amid the confusion and perplexities of this life,
help us to see the constant theme of your loving care.
In anxiety show us your provision,
in loneliness show us your company
and in uncertainty show us your wisdom,
that we may taste in this life
the fruits of your faithfulness
and the foretaste of that contentment
that comes when you are our all in all,
through Jesus Christ our Lord.

The companionship of God – seeing God in all things

Lord, we pray for your Church, that through our worship and our service, our love for you would deepen each day.

Lord of life,
who through your word bring all things into being
and through your love bring all things to fulfilment,
bless us as we seek to serve you,
that in all that we say and do and think
we may catch a glimpse of your presence,
which strengthens us on our journey
and guides us onwards on our path,
through Jesus Christ our Lord.

The companionship of God in the changing seasons of life – guidance

Lord, we pray for your Church, that in love we may flourish and grow in the joy of knowing your Son.

God of beginnings and of endings,
God of growth and of struggle,
be with us through the changing experiences of our lives.
When we lose our way direct us,
when we are open to new horizons encourage us,
when we need your stillness and your gentleness calm us,
that through all this pilgrimage of life
we may know you as the goal for which we long,
and as our companion on the way,
in Jesus Christ our Lord.

The companionship of God brings us peace and enables us to support others

Lord, we pray for your Church, that we would help the world to find peace and strength in your love.

God of peace,
in whose love our hope of rest abides,
be present with us in the changes and anxieties of this earthly life
and, through the compassion you give us for others,
enable us to hold before them the light of hope
and the reassurance of support and fellowship in times of difficulty,
through Jesus Christ our Lord.

The companionship of God – finding God in a time of difficulty

God of kindness, we pray that we may know you in our darkest times, that when we feel lost you would make yourself known in the small things of life and in the love of others.

God of peace,
when times are difficult you show us your presence in the simple
    things of life.
Amid the suffering and pain of today,
help us to know your life in the beauty of nature,
your joy in the gift of food and drink,
your friendship in a conversation with a friend
and your love in those small acts of kindness we can do for
    one another,
that in all this we may find you,
O God from whom we can never be parted,
in Jesus Christ our Lord.

The Pilgrimage of Life

The pilgrimage of life – citizens of both earth and heaven

God of our journey, we pray for your guidance on our path
through life, that in you we may know direction, encouragement,
comfort and peace.

O God of us all,
you call us to live as citizens of this earth,
but also to rejoice in our citizenship of heaven.
Lead us, we pray, on the pilgrimage of this life
that we may work for the good of our human communities,
and be made ready to attain the life of your kingdom,
through Jesus Christ our Lord.

The pilgrimage of life – growth in grace

Lord, we pray for your Church, that guided by your Holy Spirit
we would do all those things you desire and open our hearts daily
more and more to your love.

God our guide,
your light shows us the path we should walk
and your love sustains us on the journey.
Be with us in the pilgrimage of our lives,
that in all moments of loneliness we would know your presence,
in all moments of uncertainty we would know your direction
and in all moments of pain we would know your peace,
through the one who came to walk alongside us as our friend,
even Jesus Christ our Lord.

The pilgrimage of life (Baptism and Confirmation) – eyes fixed on home

Lord, we pray for your Church, that knowing our home to be in heaven we would live lives worthy of your calling [and we pray especially today for those who are to be confirmed, that as God has led them safely to this moment, so he would continue to lead them on in the adventure of life].

Lord God,
you have called us to be a people in pilgrimage
and made our whole life to be a journey towards you.
Bless us on our way,
that with our eyes fixed on the promised land of our
    heavenly home
we may find encouragement, joy and peace in this life,
as we dare to discover more of what it is you want each one of us
    to be,
this day and always,
through Jesus Christ our Lord.

The Guidance of God

The guidance of God – show us how to live

Lord, we pray for your guidance throughout our lives, that in all
that we do we would be led closer to your undying love.

Lord of all wisdom, we pray for your Church.
As we seek you in our prayers and in the actions of our daily lives,
grant us the insight to see the path you have laid ahead for us.
Where the way seems unclear, grant us your light to know
    where to tread,
where the way seems difficult, give us your courage to follow it,
where the way seems unending, give us your steadfastness
    to persevere,
that at the last we may come to that eternal city,
which you have prepared for us all to dwell in,
the city of peace and the home of all true delights,
through Jesus Christ our Lord.

The guidance of God – give us wisdom in all that we do

Lord of all truth, grant us your gift of wisdom, that in all our
words and actions we may follow in your ways.

God of all,
by whose wisdom the world was made in the beginning
and by whose inspiration
human beings are led to fashion things of beauty, truth
and goodness, enlighten our minds, we pray,
that in listening and in speaking, in teaching and in learning,
in caring and in being served
we may come to understand more deeply, ourselves, our world
and you our God, in Jesus Christ our Lord.

The guidance of God – direct our steps

Lord our God, be our light on our path, that knowing you as our guide we may find our way to our true home with you.

O Lord God,
you call all things back to yourself,
through Jesus Christ, the king of all.
Be with each one of us on our journey through life,
that however wandering, all our paths may be directed
  towards you,
and grant us faithful friends and wise counsellors to guide us
as fellow pilgrims on the journey that leads us home,
through the same Jesus Christ our Lord.

The guidance of God – Christ our light

Lord of light, shine in our darkness, that by your radiance we may know the truth of your will for our lives.

Lord God,
whose Son Jesus Christ is the bright morning star,
shed the light of your truth on all that is within us that needs your
  illumination.
Show us where we have gone astray,
teach us your calling on our lives
and help us, most of all, to know more of you,
that we would find in you our peace and our joy,
through Jesus Christ our Lord.

The guidance of God – light in darkness

Lord, we pray for your Church, that we may live in the light of your eternal day.

God of light,
in whom there is no darkness nor shadow of change,
in all the tribulations and struggles of our lives be our
    equal brightness.
In times of perplexity give us your guidance,
in times of despair give us your hope,
in times of conflict give us your peace,
that, enflamed by your powerful grace,
we may offer through our actions a hymn of praise to you
and, with thankful hearts, may know our lives to be filled with
    your gifts,
through Jesus Christ our Lord.

The guidance of God – the light brings guidance in confusion

Lord, bless your Church, that in the light of Christ all our ways
would be made clear.

Lord God,
you are our guide on our journey through life
and the light on our way.
Shine, we pray, in all places of darkness of our lives,
that in all our confusions we may know your guidance,
in all our doubts we may know your hope
and in all our loneliness we may know your company and
    your peace,
through Jesus Christ our Lord.

The guidance of God – self-knowledge and service

Lord, we pray for your Church, that seeing the truth of ourselves
and one another we would act with justice and integrity this and
every day.

God of justice,
you know better than ourselves the thoughts of our hearts.
In your mercy teach us your righteousness
and in your grace allow us to be gentle with ourselves,
that, enlightened by your Spirit,
our souls may be day by day won to your service in cheerfulness
    and joy,
through Jesus Christ our Lord.

The guidance of God – the wisdom of God

Lord, we pray for your Church, that guided by your wisdom
we may serve you with righteousness and gentleness this day
and always.

God of truth,
your wisdom is the light by which we know your will
and the guide by which we come to follow in your way.
Renew our minds by your Holy Spirit,
that we may see with all clarity
the actions you would have us do,
the words you would have us speak
and the friends you would have us know,
in Jesus Christ our Lord.

The guidance of God – guide us with your wisdom

God our creator, open our minds to the wisdom of your ways,
that seeking you in love we may follow you in lives of goodness.

God of all,
by whose wisdom the earth was fashioned
and the rich variety of its creatures was made,
bless our hearts with your gift of understanding.
Guide us in our times of uncertainty,
teach us the ways of righteousness
and show us the call you have on our lives,
that in faith, in courage and in perseverance
we may follow where you lead
and bring your love to our world,
through Jesus Christ our Lord.

The guidance of God – our purpose and vocation

God our guide, be with us in all our times of difficulty,
that however great our struggles we may know that we are
never alone.

God, you know us from our creation
and you understand our nature before we are born.
Bless us in our searching for your will for our lives.
Help us to hear the voice of your call when our lives seem empty
    and you seem far away,
and grant us the courage to follow the path of service you have
    laid before each one of us
and to find in it meaning, peace and joy,
through Jesus Christ our Lord.

Part 2 Prayers for the Life of the Church

The guidance of God – help us to hear your call

Lord, we pray for your Church, that in all our doings we may not lose sight of Christ at the centre of our lives.

Lord of all,
in whom we live and move and have our being,
renew our hearts through your Holy Spirit,
that we may long to draw close to you in prayer,
that we may have the faith to hear your call on our lives
and that we may have the courage to tread the path you have set
    before us,
through Jesus Christ our Lord.

The guidance of God in the life of the Church

Let us pray for the Church, for our flourishing and growth in understanding and in love.

Lord of all creation,
bless the work of your Church.
In our worship be our inspiration,
in our thinking be our guide,
in our service be our example and forerunner,
in our prayer be our companion
and in our lives be our friend,
through Jesus Christ our Lord.

Discipleship

Faithfulness to our Calling

Christian commitment – call us out of our complacency

Lord, we pray for your Church, that we may seek you all our days.

Loving God,
the desire of those who seek you
and the joy of those who find you,
call us this day out of our apathy and complacency
towards the vision of your kingdom.
Strengthen our hope,
renew our zeal
and deepen our love,
for the sake of Jesus Christ our Lord.

Christian commitment – refresh us in tiredness and inspire us in despair

Lord, we pray for your Church, that refreshed and renewed we would serve you in our lives with new life and vigour.

Lord whose love is never-ending
and whose promises to us are full of hope,
refresh us in times of tiredness
and renew us in moments of despair,
that we may learn to see our lives with the fullness of your vision,
where cheerfulness and sorrow, anger and excitement, complaint
    and praise are enfolded
in the arms of one all-encompassing love,
in Jesus Christ our Lord.

Discipleship – seeking God in prayer, worship and study

God our guide and our goal, teach us to seek you in all that we do, that as we experience something of your glory and your love each day, we may know how much remains for us to discover and enjoy.

Lord God,
your delight is to be with us
and you have taught us that our only joy comes when we are
    with you.
Help us to know your presence in every passing moment of
    our lives,
teach us to seek you more urgently in prayer, in worship and in
    study of the Scriptures,
and grant that we may minister peace, comfort and reconciliation
    to others in your name,
through Jesus Christ our Lord.

Discipleship – faithfulness

Lord, we thank you for the gift of your Church, to encourage us in our faith, to deepen us in our love for one another and to enable us to serve more effectively the needs of the world.

Lord of all life,
you created all things in the beginning and said they were good,
and have called each one of us to participate in the even greater
    glories of the new creation
in Jesus Christ your Son.
In the midst of all the busyness and distractions of this world,
grant us your grace to hold fast to you,
that our spirits may be strengthened,
our decisions and plans may be guided
and our hearts may be enlarged,
through your Son, Jesus Christ our Lord.

Discipleship – faithful to our calling

Lord, we pray for your Church, that you would renew each one
of us with your love and your peace.

Lord God,
we thank you for your calling to be disciples of your Son.
Stir up within us, we pray, the many gifts of your Spirit,
that through all our actions and all our words
we would reflect your love to the world,
and through our characters and our lives
others would be drawn to hunger for the truth of the gospel
    for themselves,
through Jesus Christ our Lord.

Discipleship – integrity in faith

Lord of all, we pray for your Church, that it would be truly a
house of prayer for all the nations. Help all Christians to live out
our faith with integrity and with compassion to others. Keep us
from all self-righteousness and pride, and prevent us from seeking
to manipulate your gifts of faith and worship to justify our
prejudices or for our own selfish gain.

Heavenly Father,
we thank you for the gift of life in the Spirit in the holy Church
    of Christ.
Grant us anew your grace,
that we may love you as you love us,
without selfishness, without ulterior motive and without desire
    for gain,
that our worship may be pure,
our prayers honest
and our lives upright in your sight,
through Jesus Christ our Lord.

Discipleship – fullness of life

Lord God, in whose mercy we are given words to speak of
you, songs to praise you and hearts to love you, we pray for
our Church.

Holy God,
you call your people together
in a fellowship of love, hope and truth.
Bless all those who seek to serve you in the life of your Church,
that through our common witness to the gospel
the whole world may come to know the joy of a life fully lived in
the presence of God,
through Jesus Christ our Lord.

Discipleship – seeking God

Lord, we pray for your Church, that inspired by your love and
drawn together in unity we may preach your gospel to a world
in need.

God of eternity,
whose salvation is known from generation to generation,
bless those who seek you this day,
that by discovering more of your truth
we may learn more deeply the meaning of love,
and by imitating the example of your Son
we may know the fulfilment that is found in serving others,
through the same Jesus Christ our Lord.

Discipleship – transformation

Lord, we pray for your Church, that our hearts would be
refreshed and our spirits renewed in our service of you and of one
another.

Lord of creation,
without you nothing can flourish and nothing can be holy.
Pour out afresh your Spirit on our Church this day,
that our doubt may be transformed into hope,
our fear may be transformed into excitement
and our despondency may be transformed into joy,
through Jesus Christ our Lord.

Discipleship – transformation by the light of Christ

Lord, we pray for your Church, that your light of beauty, truth
and goodness would flood through our thoughts, our words and
our deeds.

God of all,
whose Son came among us as the light of the world,
bestow on your Church your gifts,
that our eyes may be opened to see your light,
our lives transformed by its radiance
and our world healed by the warmth of our generosity and love,
through Jesus Christ our Lord.

Our Discipleship Leading to Service of our World

Discipleship – faithful in prayer and active in service

Lord, teach us to pray and strengthen us to serve, that the world
may know your love within us.

God of our calling,
you have summoned us to serve the world with generosity
and to know that in serving others we are serving your Son.
Strengthen all those who follow your way
to remain faithful in prayer and active in service,
that many in our world may experience the gift of your love,
in Jesus Christ our Lord.

Discipleship – our life in the Church prepares us to serve the world

Lord, bless your Church, that we may preach your word to the
whole earth.

Lord, in the fellowship of your Church
you give us life and purpose
and show us the meaning of true joy and hope.
Enrich our worship and our fellowship by the quickening gift of
    your Holy Spirit,
that we may be inspired to new devotion in prayer
and new diligence in our care of others,
through Jesus Christ our Lord.

Discipleship – the Christian calling

Lord, we pray for all Christians, that as we draw closer to you
so we may grow closer to those around us.

Give grace, O Lord, to all members of your Church,
whatever their calling,
that strengthened by the study of the Scriptures and the
    celebration of the sacraments
we may be deep in understanding, bold in proclamation,
loving in service and persistent in prayer,
through Jesus Christ our Lord.

Discipleship – empowered by the Spirit

Lord, inflame our hearts with the gift of your Spirit, that we may
serve you with joy.

Lord of life,
whose Spirit moved on the face of the waters in creation
and came with power on the Church at Pentecost,
quicken us in all that we do in your service.
Make our worship sincere,
our service compassionate
and our preaching full of conviction,
that the world may come to experience that faith, that hope and
    that love
which you have made known to us,
in Jesus Christ our Lord.

Discipleship – may our lives glorify you

Lord, we pray for your Church, that we may sing your praise in
all our words and in all our deeds.

God of all,
who gave us hearts to love you,
lips to praise you
and lives to follow you,
direct us in all that we do,
that we may come to know you in prayer,
glorify you in worship
and serve you in action,
this and every day,
through Jesus Christ our Lord.

Discipleship – *awe at our creation*

Lord, we pray for your Church, that seeking you with all our
heart we may come to know you in the love and service of others.

Creator of the stars of the heavens,
who fashioned human beings as the crown of your creation
and human hearts as the object of your longing,
fill us, who gaze on the wonders you have made,
with such awe that we may know your glory,
such love that we may know your care
and such understanding that we may offer your wisdom to others,
through one who, being God,
entered into the created world for its salvation,
even Jesus Christ our Lord.

Discipleship – *daily renewal*

Lord, we pray for your Church, that together we may grow in
faith, hope and love.

Lord of all,
through your power you created us in the beginning
and through your love you call us back to you each day.
Open our hearts to the promptings of your Spirit,
that our lives would be filled with your peace, your joy and
    your righteousness,
through Jesus Christ our Lord.

Discipleship – the gift of the Church

Lord, we pray for your Church, that you would renew us in understanding, in compassion and in zeal for the good news.

Lord of all the world,
we thank you for the gift of your Church,
for the teaching we receive through it,
for the fellowship we obtain within it
and for the glory we experience in its worship.
Strengthen us in our calling as your disciples,
that through all we do
your love would be experienced
and your truth would be known,
through Jesus Christ our Lord.

Discipleship – learning from one another

Lord, we thank you for the gift of your Church, as a place where we grow in faith in you and in fellowship with one another.

Lord of all,
we thank you for your gift of sisters and brothers in faith,
and for the ways they teach, inspire and challenge us in our
    following of you.
Renew us by the power of your Spirit, we pray,
that our whole lives may be an offering in your service.
Take from all Christians our tendency to self-focus
    and complacency,
and open our hearts to love and serve the world you have made,
through Jesus Christ our Lord.

Discipleship – lights in the darkness

Lord God, make us to shine with your radiance, that the world may see in us the reflection of your glory.

Lord of light,
we thank you for your calling to us to shine as lights in the world.
Help us to know your presence in times of darkness,
re-invigorate us when faith seems dim and hope is failing
and help our words, our deeds and our whole beings
to be reflections of that pure light
that shines into the world, in Jesus Christ our Lord.

Discipleship – lights in the darkness, bringing hope and healing

God of all, help us to minister your love and healing to our broken world.

Lord of all light,
in whom there is no darkness at all,
enlighten, we pray, all those who profess the name of your Son
with your wisdom, your gentleness and your kindness,
that we in turn may shine as lights in the world.
Help us to bring your hope and healing
to all places of division and despair,
and give us your grace,
that in our service of others
we may work your goodness and faithfulness in our
    own communities,
through Jesus Christ our Lord.

Discipleship – children of light

Lord, we pray for your Church, that your light would be known amid all the darkness of this world.

God of all,
whose Son, Jesus Christ, is the light of the world,
banish all darkness from our hearts, we pray,
that set free from greed, indifference and cruelty
we may live as children of light,
kindling hope, comfort and grace among all those with whom we
    share our lives,
through Jesus Christ our Lord.

Discipleship – Christian education

Lord, we pray for our world. As we give thanks for the gifts
we enjoy in this place, we pray for all teachers and tutors who
develop those gifts in others; for all those whose work is to
provide guidance and care to the young; and for all those who
bring up children as parents and guardians.

God of all,
we thank you for the gift of learning,
for the joy of discovery
and for the excitement inspiring others brings.
As we seek your direction through the Scriptures, the sacraments
    and our prayers,
so help us all to guide others into ways that are fruitful,
    productive and just,
that knowing their needs and the wisdom you bring
we may, through words of kindness and lives of integrity,
teach them the skills to thrive,
the confidence to create
and the compassion to put their talents first to the service of others,
in the name of Jesus Christ our Lord.

The Call to Serve Others

Service – building a world that reflects God's glory

Lord, we pray for your Church, that we would follow in the way
of your commandments, in paths of peace and justice.

God our Creator,
you teach us that our purpose is to serve one another as you have
    served us in Jesus Christ.
Keep from our hearts all selfishness and cruelty,
that by following in the way you have set before us
we would build a world that reflects your glory and
    your compassion,
through the same Jesus Christ our Lord.

Service – doers not merely hearers (St James the Great)

God of all, [as we celebrate the feast of St James the Great, apostle
and martyr, so] we pray for your Church, that our commitment
may be deepened and our preaching refreshed.

God of truth,
through our mercy you bring us to faith
and through the example of your Son we are inspired to
    good works.
Teach us who have received your promises
to be doers of the word and not merely hearers of it,
that our faith may be alive and flourish in deeds of love,
    generosity and compassion,
through the encouragement of Jesus Christ our Lord.

Service – purify our hearts

Lord, we pray for your Church, that watching and waiting we
may seek you in prayer and service.

God our Father,
who looked on the world in love
and brought us healing and truth in your Son,
dispel from our hearts the darkness of violence and the
    cloudedness of indifference,
that we would shine as lights
in lives of integrity, words of encouragement and communities
    of hope,
through the same Jesus Christ our Lord.

Service – purify our hearts to praise you with our lives

Lord, we pray for your Church, that our whole lives may be a chorus of praise to you.

God of all creation,
who fashioned the world to be in harmony
and whose heaven resounds with the joyful music of your praise,
tune our hearts,
that in all our words, deeds and relationships
we may convey to others the beautiful echo of your love,
through Jesus Christ our Lord.

Service – a reflection of God's love

Lord, we pray for your Church, that inspired by your love we may serve a world so greatly in need.

God of our ancestors,
whose faithfulness endures from generation to generation
and whose love reaches to the ends of the earth,
grant us your grace,
that in serving others as you serve us
we may remain steadfast in commitment and generous in our care,
that the world would glimpse in our actions
a reflection of your constancy and tenderness,
through Jesus Christ our Lord.

Service – a voice for the voiceless

Lord God, we give thanks for the gifts you have given us. Help us to use them always in the service of those in need.

Lord of all,
whose Son Jesus Christ spoke of the coming of a kingdom of
    righteousness and peace
and inaugurated that new creation in the life of the Church,
we pray that we may be found faithful
to such a precious inheritance, and to such a high calling,
by being people who work for peace in our world,
people who make heard the voices of the downtrodden
    and oppressed,
people who go out of their way to befriend the poor, the stranger
    and the lost,
that in our shared life together
the world may see the pattern of the life of your Son,
Jesus Christ our Lord.

Learning God's Lesson of Love

Love – grant us your gift of love

Lord, we pray for your Church, that through the conviction of our words and the integrity of our deeds we may show the power and the love of God to those with whom we share our lives.

Almighty God,
your Son taught us that the greatest commandment is to love you
    and to love one another.
Grant us your gift of love, we pray,
that we may be led from the darkness of self-obsession
to the light of mutual care and fellowship,
lived out in friendship with Jesus Christ our Lord.

Love – God's truest name is love

Lord, we pray for your Church, that we would be filled with the love that reaches out to the love of Christ.

O God,
whose truest name is love
and whose most intimate being is in relationship,
of your kindness, share with our human hearts some of that gift
    of your love,
that, our minds and souls renewed,
we would look on you, one another and ourselves
with lovers' eyes of delight,
and find in a life shared in love
the purpose of our existence and the spring of all joy,
in Jesus Christ our Lord.

Love – make us love and teach us how

Lord, we pray for your Church, that we would be enabled to bring the light of your love into all the places of darkness of this world.

God of light,
in doubt you are our guide
and in desolation you are our comfort.
Bring your illumination to our understanding
and your warmth to our hearts,
that radiant with your hope
we would bring love and compassion
to a world so much in need,
through Jesus Christ our Lord.

Evangelism

All Christians as Evangelists

Evangelism – being apostles

God of all, we pray for your Church, that we may preach the gospel joyfully in all our words and actions.

Lord of all,
inspired by your word and your love,
your apostles preached the good news to all the peoples of
    the earth.
Strengthen us to be apostles in our own lives,
that through the goodness of our actions,
the thoughtfulness of our faith
and the quality of our common life,
many would come to know something of the joy of life with you,
in Jesus Christ our Lord.

Evangelism – creativity in evangelism

God our glory, be with us in our listening and in our speaking,
that through our attention to your voice we would be enabled to
witness to your truth with honesty and integrity in our world.

Lord of all,
we thank you that in Jesus Christ you came alongside us
to teach us love and strengthen us in faith.
Be with us all, we pray, as we seek to follow you,
that through our discussions and our encouragement of
   one another
we may learn more of your truth
and have the energy and the courage
to serve this world in new and imaginative ways,
that through your gift of creativity,
your holy gospel would be preached afresh in our generation,
through Jesus Christ our Lord.

Evangelism – by loving action

Let us pray for the Church, that in all our worship and our action
in the world, God's love would be made known.

Almighty Father,
in your redeeming love you have drawn us together
into this community of worship and service.
Deepen our love for you, we pray,
and grant that by our faithfulness in prayer and through the
   quality of our common life,
others may be drawn towards your truth
and discover your joy in their lives,
through Jesus Christ our Lord.

Evangelism – through thoughtful faith and deeds of integrity

Heavenly Father, we pray for the renewal of all Christian life, that each one of us might preach the gospel in our every word and action.

Lord of life,
you have called us into the mystical body of your Son
and have given us your Holy Spirit to strengthen us to share the
    good news with others.
Refresh us in our confidence in the gospel
and our love for our fellow women and men,
that through the thoughtfulness of our faith
and the conviction of our deeds,
many would come to know your presence and your care,
in Jesus Christ our Lord.

Evangelism – show the world the hope, joy and peace of Christ

God of hope, make us so to fall in love with your truth, that we would seek to speak of it to the ends of the earth.

God of all,
you call us together to worship you
and to be seekers after your truth in our lives.
Strengthen all those who strive to preach your gospel and live by
    your teachings
in this and every nation,
that together we may show to our world
the hope, the joy and the peace
of Jesus Christ our Lord.

Evangelism – in this land

Lord, bless this land, that in it your truth would be known and
your love would be shared.

Lord of all,
through the life of the Trinity you show us the power of a
    unified love.
Strengthen all of us who seek to serve you in this land,
that we may preach the gospel with boldness,
that we may reach out to those in need with compassion
and that we may grow together in mutual understanding
    and fellowship,
through Jesus Christ our Lord.

Evangelism – through our lives

Lord, we pray for your Church, that strengthened by Christ we
may proclaim his love to the world.

God of love,
whose Son gave up his life that we might live,
direct us in all that we do in his name,
that through us our families, our friends and all those we meet
would come to know within themselves
that spring of water which wells up to eternal life,
in Jesus Christ our Lord.

Evangelism – show your glory in our lives

Lord, we pray for your Church, that through lives of goodness we
would reveal your glory to our world.

God of glory,
by your will the whole creation came into being,
and by your love it is sustained and flourishes with delight.
Show us your glory in our lives,
that through the beauty of all that is around us
we would come to know your majesty,
and through our words and actions
we would come to share the inspiration you bring with others,
through Jesus Christ our Lord.

Evangelism in words and deeds

Lord, we pray for your Church, that as we speak of your noble
acts we would call the whole world to come and worship you and
glorify your name.

God of the ages,
in whom are all the perfections of peace,
send on your Church the renewing power of your Spirit,
that our words may help others to know your truth,
our actions may help others to know your love
and our relationships may help others to know your friendship
    and your encouragement,
in Jesus Christ our Lord.

Missionaries & Evangelists

Evangelists

Lord of all, we pray for your Church, for our life in the world and our witness to the gospel of your Son.

Almighty God,
you breathed the life of the Spirit into your Church at Pentecost,
that the good news of your Son might be known throughout
   the world.
Bless, we pray, those who preach the gospel
with powerful words and generous actions in our own day,
renew them with your wisdom and your strength
and teach us all how best to serve you so that the world
   might believe,
through Jesus Christ our Lord.

Evangelists – following in the footsteps of the missionaries

God of all, we pray for your Church. [On this day when we remember the missionary N,] we pray for all Christians in this land, that we may preach the gospel joyfully in all our words and actions.

Lord of all,
inspired by your word and your love,
your missionaries preached the good news to all the peoples of the
   earth.
Strengthen us to be missionaries in our own lives,
that through the goodness of our actions,
the thoughtfulness of our faith
and the quality of our common life,
many would come to know something of the joy of life with you,
in Jesus Christ our Lord.

Service & Public Good

Service & public good

Lord, teach us to love to serve others, that in seeking their good
above our own we may discover our purpose and our own
true selves.

Heavenly Father,
who called your Church to be your presence in the world,
renew us in the love that you have shown to us in Jesus Christ,
so that by serving the hungry, the thirsty, the naked, the strangers
    and the prisoners,
we may know ourselves to be serving your Son,
and, through this service,
your kingdom of justice, righteousness and peace
may be ever more visible in our troubled world,
through the same Jesus Christ our Lord.

Service & public good – may we bring healing and reconciliation

Lord, we pray for your Church, that knowing your light in our lives we may help others to see it in a world of darkness and confusion.

Lord God, hope of the nations,
whose Son came as the light of the world
to show us the image of love
and to teach us the ways of peace,
nurture in our hearts the hope he brings,
that in a world of suffering, uncertainty and cruelty
we may be people of healing, wisdom and hope,
that in ways large and small
we may show to others the reflection of that reconciliation
we have ourselves received,
in Jesus Christ our Lord.

Service & public good – the Church's influence on society

Lord of all the world, bless your Church, that we may speak to the world words of truth, integrity and peace.

God of all,
you call us to preach your justice in our world
and to show the ways of righteousness by lives lived in your love.
Guide your Church, as we work together across traditions
    and cultures,
to speak your word in the public square.
Keep us from the temptations of easy answers and smugness,
teach us to say what is true, not what wins applause,
and through it all give us such compassion
that we may speak for those whose voices so often go unheard,
and assist them in finding hope and fair treatment,
through Jesus Christ our Lord.

Service & public good – collaboration with civil society

Lord, we pray for your Church, that through our work we may be
a blessing to all those with whom we share our lives.

Almighty God,
you call us together
to live our lives in community with others.
Bless the ministry of your Church,
that through working in partnership with all people of good will
we may bring the love of Christ more effectively to a world so
    much in need,
through the same Jesus Christ our Lord.

Service & public good – in a time of public difficulty

Lord, direct your Church in these difficult times, that we
may know how best to speak and act for the good of our
whole society.

God of all,
you inspire your Church with the Holy Spirit
to be filled with a love of service
and an insight into how we may best serve your world.
In the uncertainty and rapid changes of these days,
show us how to be your light in times of darkness,
your refreshment in times of thirst
and your healing in times of distress,
through Jesus Christ our Lord.

PART 3

Prayers for the Life of the World

The Environment

The environment – justice for the world and one another

Heavenly Father, we give you thanks for the beauty of this natural
world. We pray for a better relationship between humanity and
the rest of your creation, for all those who work in agriculture,
for those who work in conservation and for all governments and
those forming environmental policy, that they may be inspired
by the responsibility you have laid on us to be stewards of your
creation.

O God,
you fashioned us to live in harmony
with the world you have made.
Deepen our respect for the gift of your creation,
that working with the earth
in ways that are sustainable,
we may provide enough
to feed all the peoples of this planet
now and for generations to come,
through Jesus Christ our Lord.

The environment – commitment to its service

Lord, we pray for your world. We pray that we may re-commit ourselves to caring for this planet, that it may be a place of safety and beauty for all its inhabitants today and for all those who come after us.

God of love,
who formed this planet to be the environment in which we
   can flourish
and who charged us to be stewards of this nurturing home for the
   generations to come,
grant us your care as we interact with the nature you have made.
Teach us sensitivity to the world's needs,
grant us moderation in living in ways that are sustainable
and show us how best to collaborate with one another,
that through common action and shared concern
we may preserve this priceless treasure
for the sustenance of our children and those who come after them,
through Jesus Christ our Lord.

The environment – 'it is very good'

Lord, we pray for your world. We pray especially today for our stewardship of all your creation. We give thanks for the beauty and the fruitfulness of the land and for the work and care of those who labour on it, and we pray that we would use this gift responsibly, enabling it to flourish both for us and for future generations.

God of creation,
who saw the earth and said 'it is very good'
and who gave human beings the responsibility for its care and
   development,
show us how to safeguard this treasure for our children.
Keep us from the exploitation that brings short-term advantage
   to us but leaves serious damage for the future,
give us wisdom to use our skills and technologies with sensitivity
   and care,
and deepen our understanding of the wonders of your creation,
that we would know what best serves its good
and grow in wonder at its intricate beauty,
through Jesus Christ our Lord.

The environment – respect for the natural world

Creator of all things, we pray for your world, for a deeper
and more respectful relationship between humanity and the
rest of creation, for a thoughtful stewardship of our natural
environment, for the compassionate treatment of animals and for
a greater humanity to one another.

Lord of all,
you created the earth to be our home
and charged us to cultivate and care for it.
Give us in our own day
the wisdom to know what is good for our planet,
the restraint to work with the earth in ways that are sustainable
and the forethought to preserve the beauty of our environment for
    future generations,
through Jesus Christ our Lord.

The environment – Rogation

Lord, [on this Rogation Day] we pray for the fruitfulness of
the earth. We give thanks for the beauty of creation and for its
sustenance of life of all kinds, and we pray that in thankfulness
for all the world gives us we may treat it with the respect and the
care it deserves.

God of plenty,
who made the earth to yield its fruit in season
and fashioned it with a beauty that inspires us all,
grant us the gentleness to care for our planet with love,
help us to understand what is best for it,
help us to commit to preserve it for our children
and help us to nurture it, as it nurtures us,
through Jesus Christ our Lord.

The environment – thanksgiving for its fragile beauty

Lord, we pray for your world. As we give thanks for the beauty
of this day, we pray for your earth, for all those who work to
conserve it, for a right use of its natural resources and for wisdom
and restraint in our relationship with the gift of our planet.

O God, who created the world out of love
and looked on it, saying 'it is very good',
we thank you for the gift of this earth,
for the cycle of the seasons and the interdependence of life,
for its power to sustain human existence
and for its fragile beauty, which brings us such joy.
Teach us to be worthy custodians of so great a treasure,
that by nurturing your creation
and by treating it with gentleness and respect,
it may bring to those who come after us
the same nourishment and delight it has brought us for so
    many centuries,
through Jesus Christ our Lord.

THE NATIONS OF THE WORLD

Peace

Peace – shared humanity (Advent: O Rex Gentium)

Lord God, who made all the peoples of this earth, we pray for
peace among the nations. May there be renewed understanding
between peoples of different cultures and traditions, renewed
respect for the human dignity of each person and renewed
wisdom in our leaders, that together we may walk the paths
of peace.

Lord God,
whose Son Jesus Christ is the desire of the nations
and the one through whom unity and righteousness will abound
    on the earth,
teach your people the ways of peace,
that all the different peoples of this earth
may come to know that their most profound identity is founded
not on race, nation, class or wealth
but in the common humanity we all share,
the crown of your creation
and the rich treasure that binds us all together,
through the Incarnation of Jesus Christ our Lord.

Peace between nations

Lord God, have mercy on your world. We pray for good relations between the nations of the world, for greater concern for the plight of those who suffer because of political conflicts, for kindness to refugees and strangers and for a renewed commitment on the part of our leaders to work together for the flourishing and prosperity of all.

Creator of all,
you long for the harmony of the human race
and for peace between the nations.
In places of conflict bring us your healing,
in places of suffering bring us your strength,
in places of oppression bring us your protection
and in places of power bring your love and compassion,
for the sake of your Son, who endured the violence of
    hostile humanity,
even Jesus Christ our Lord.

Peace between nations – the order of God

Lord our God, we pray for your gifts of stability and wisdom in a world that seems turbulent and fragile, and for a renewed commitment on the part of all our leaders to building the confidence, trust and security that allow ordinary people to flourish.

Eternal God,
through whose mercy the whole created order is held in its place,
and through whose Spirit of unity
creatures are brought to delight in togetherness
and human community is made possible,
send your Holy Spirit on the nations of this world,
that putting aside pride, war and greed
we may reach out to one another in friendship,
and nurture within our own societies those gifts of tolerance,
    understanding and love
that bring joy to life,
in Jesus Christ our Lord.

Peace throughout the nations

Lord, we pray today for all nations and especially for places
where there is persecution, where there is violence, where there is
indifference, anxiety and alienation, that the whole world would
come to know your healing love.

King of peace,
who longs for us to live in fellowship and unity,
send your Spirit of peace throughout our world.
Take from our hearts all prejudice and envy,
take from our hands the weapons of violence
and take from our lips all words of cruelty,
that we may live as brothers and sisters,
one family in the love of your Son,
Jesus Christ our Lord.

Peace – may all people be people of peace

Lord, in our time of violence and uncertainty we pray for peace,
for an end to the pride that keeps us apart from one another, to
the prejudice that wounds our own humanity even as it denigrates
others, and to the love of dominion that is at the root of so much
of our human sin.

Lord, your Son said to his disciples,
'Peace I leave with you; my peace I give you'.
Grant, we pray, that we may be so filled with this gift
that we become people of peace in a world of violence.
Teach the leaders of the nations to pursue peace with one another,
show us all the value of those different from ourselves
and draw us together into one family of peace, as your children in
    the world,
through Jesus Christ our Lord.

Peace – give us hearts that seek peace

Lord, we pray for peace in our world, that, laying aside the
violence of our hearts, we may work together for a world in
which all people can flourish.

God of love,
in whom we are all united,
bring together in your peace all the nations of this world.
Keep us from the temptations of blame and aggression
to which our human struggle so often leads,
and help us instead to pursue the ways of
gentleness, diplomacy and understanding,
through Jesus Christ our Lord.

Peace – swords into ploughshares

Lord God, we pray for your world and we remember before you
today those many places of conflict, praying for peace between
the nations of this earth, peace within countries torn apart by
tension and civil strife, peace within homes and families, and
peace within our own hearts.

God of peace,
in whose kingdom the lion shall lie down with the lamb
and the swords shall be beaten into ploughshares,
pour into our hearts that love of peace that takes away all envy
    and strife.
Give us honesty to speak openly of our differences,
give us courage to stand up for what is right
and give us discernment that, through careful discussion and wise
    compromise,
we may bring about an order in our world and in our lives
that serves the good of all, weak and strong,
in Jesus Christ our Lord.

Peace through dialogue (Pentecost)

Lord, we pray for your world. [On this Pentecost day,] we pray
for the unity of the peoples, for greater mutual understanding and
for a renewed desire for dialogue with one another.

King of kings,
whose Spirit brings order, unity and concord to all creation,
bring together the divided nations of this world,
that through loving one another
and through respectful dialogue about our disagreements,
all your children may be led to become people of peace,
people of honesty and people of hope,
in Jesus Christ our Lord.

Peace – the peace of Jerusalem and the Holy Land

Lord God, we pray for your world, and in particular for the
peace of the holy city of Jerusalem and the Holy Land, for a sense
of unity and deep mutual understanding between the different
religious and cultural groups that live there, for renewed political
commitment among the leaders of Israel and Palestine to peace
and justice; and we pray for the international community, that we
may do all within our power to seek to support and facilitate the
cause of peace in that holy place.

Lord God,
we thank you for your gift of the Holy Land
and we join our voices with the voices of others throughout
    the centuries
to pray for the peace of Jerusalem.
May there be peace within her walls,
peace between Jew and Muslim and Christian,
peace between Israeli and Palestinian,
peace between rich and poor,
that Jerusalem may be to the whole world
a sign of the friendship that is possible between cultures,
and of the joy of walking together in unity,
through Jesus Christ our Lord.

Peace within a divided society

Lord, we pray for your world, and especially today for leaders in
places of disunity and civil strife, for a spirit of collaboration and
trust, a willingness to compromise and a commitment to putting
the restoration of peace and good government above party
advantage and sectarian concerns.

God of love,
you call us together into unity
and ask us to seek, through the insight our differences give us,
the common good of all.
Bless all those who serve the people of N,
draw them into dialogue,
sustain their trust
and deepen their love for one another,
that amid all their diversity of politics
they may know the human dignity they share
and desire to support the flourishing of all who live in
    their communities,
for the sake of Jesus Christ our Lord.

Unity

Unity – in all places of conflict (All Saints' Day)

Lord, we pray for our world, for all those many places of conflict
and disagreement. Help us to know that with all our differences
of opinion and politics we are called to be one holy people, one
company of saints amid all the fractures of the world.

Lord, in the fellowship of the saints
you show us how a profound diversity of character and experience
can bear fruit in a glorious unity of purpose and love.
Teach us, we pray, to harness our own differences
so that we may grow into ever deeper insight,
ever greater unity
and ever more effective service of all your creatures,
through Jesus Christ our Lord.

Unity – those in danger

Lord, we pray for your world, for all places where there is discord and division, where there are broken relationships and a lack of trust. We pray for those for whom home is not a safe or comforting place, for those for whom venturing outside puts them at risk, for those who find society indifferent to their sufferings or hostile to their very existence.

Lord of all truth,
you made the world for joy
and yet we have made it a place of fear;
you made human beings for fellowship
and yet so often we choose division.
Bring once again, we pray, your gift of harmony to our
    broken communities,
that knowing you as our guide,
and our neighbours as brothers and sisters,
we may join together in understanding and in mutual respect,
to become a chorus of hope for a world so much in need,
through Jesus Christ our Lord.

Unity – listening to one another in our nation

Lord God, we pray for your world. In the life of our nation, we pray for your guidance for our leaders, for wisdom and judgement among all those who stand for public office, and for our whole nation, that we may turn away from anger and divisiveness, and seek to cooperate and support one another in all that we do.

God of all peace,
by your Spirit we are drawn together into deeper understanding
   and more profound love.
Pour out your healing on our tense and divided nation,
that as we know your tender care for us,
so we may learn to be gentle with those around us,
that by hearing their voices, and by speaking with wisdom
   and honesty,
we may come to a shared purpose and a clearer vision of where
   our future lies,
knowing that all our ways are known to you and held in the love
   of your Son,
Jesus Christ our Lord.

Unity – inspire the world with your love

Lord, we pray for your world, that amid the darkness and
confusion, the light of truth and hope would be known.

God of light,
in you there is no darkness
and without you there is no hope.
Shine the beam of your love into our troubled world.
Teach all of us the openness to hear your voice in the words
   of others,
and grant us the discernment to seek that path
which will lead us towards the justice, unity and fairness
that is your will for our world,
in Jesus Christ our Lord.

Unity – international cooperation through shared work

Lord, we pray for your world. We pray for all institutions and projects that bring people of different nationalities to work together for the common good, for the work of the United Nations and all international organizations, for charities, businesses, academic and arts establishments, and all those places where people of different backgrounds share their enthusiasm and their effort in pursuit of a shared goal.

Generous God,
you reveal to us, in others, that great unity which all human
    beings share,
and in the connections we make with one another
we come to know your loving presence, which crosses all frontiers.
Be with your children in all our shared endeavours,
that we would learn from the insights that others bring,
create a better future for those who come after us
and, by the relationships our work builds up,
draw together ever more powerfully all the peoples of this earth
into your one family of love,
through one who is your Son
yet did not hesitate to become our brother,
even Jesus Christ our Lord.

Unity – love not hate

Lord, we pray for your world. We pray for unity and peace within our own society, for good relations between peoples of different cultural backgrounds and for a flourishing of all work that promotes greater mutual understanding, and greater shared life. We pray for our schools and colleges, that they may teach a new generation the values of tolerance and respect, and for all who lead our society, that they may act with integrity, fairness and a greater concern for doing right than for public opinion.

Lord, our God,
in whose kingdom righteousness and justice alone are known,
look with mercy, we pray, on the life of this world.
Where people are hurting, bring your comfort,
where people are divided, bring your unity,
where people are angry, fearful and cruel, bring your calm,
that together we may come to learn the beauty of that harmony
which is your will for all peoples,
in your Son, Jesus Christ our Lord.

Unity – promoting harmony not division

Lord, we pray for your world. As we hear of attempts, almost each day, to gain power by encouraging hostilities and increasing division, we pray for the many gifts of your Spirit of peace. We pray for the grace to welcome others as we would wish to welcome Christ, for greater respect and understanding among all peoples of the legitimacy of different opinions, and for a renewed commitment among the leaders of the nations to seek to heal and not to destroy.

Father of all people,
bring healing to your family,
divided against one another by jealousy, anger and pride.
Break down those barriers we have created between ourselves,
remove our indifference to the suffering of those who are different
and help us all to see one another with your eyes of love,
that we may know ourselves to be brothers and sisters once again,
through Jesus Christ our Lord.

Unity – cooperation not cynicism

Lord, we pray for your world. In an age of anger and negativity, we pray for a change in our public discourse, for a love of truth, for a commitment to working together and for a recognition of the dignity and the integrity of others.

Lord of all,
you call us to bear one another's burdens
and to show kindness in the face of another's weakness.
Teach us to turn away from our culture of cynicism and scorn,
to reject the way of insult and point-scoring
and to seek instead the path of humility,
that through listening, cooperation and wise discussion
we may work together to build a future more just, more hopeful
    and more full of peace
than any of us could imagine alone,
through Jesus Christ our Lord.

Unity – respect for, not jealousy, of others

Lord of all, we pray for your world, broken apart by jealousy, envy and pride. Help us and all people not to be jealous of the talents or the prominence of others, but guide us in the way of peace, that we may learn through cherishing, encouraging and promoting others, to truly love ourselves for who we are.

Lord of peace,
you love all people with one equal love,
yet knowledge of such love is almost more than we can bear.
In our human insecurity,
keep us from the idolatry of wealth, status, power
    or respectability,
that we may come to know that by sharing and by serving
we do not lose what we have
but rather are set free to receive all you have to offer us,
through Jesus Christ our Lord.

Unity – finding joy in diversity
(Week of prayer for Christian Unity)

Lord, [as we pray for Christian Unity, so] we pray for unity in our world, our national life and our own communities. We pray for an end to the barriers of prejudice that keep people apart, the fear that makes us attack so as not to be hurt, and the divisions created by political leaders which cause such great suffering, that we may all seek peace and happiness together as one human family.

God of all peoples,
your love stretches beyond all ages
and your care extends beyond all space.
Bring your healing, we pray, to the fractures of this broken world.
Bind up what is wounded in our societies and in our hearts
and renew our spirits,
that we may find delight in difference
and refreshment in those who are unlike us,
through Jesus Christ our Lord.

Unity – the value of the good of all and the uniqueness of each

Lord of all, we pray for unity throughout the world, that recognizing the different gifts each one of us has to offer we may share our talents for the good of all.

God of peace,
whose will is for the whole world to find our reconciliation in you,
draw together people of different nations and politics through
   your infinite love,
that knowing one another as brothers and sisters in our
   human family
we may work together for the good of all
while upholding the uniqueness of each,
and may be drawn into greater unity
while rejoicing in the richness of our distinctiveness,
through one whose will and work reach beyond all barriers,
even Jesus Christ our Lord.

Unity – the Commonwealth

Lord, we pray for our world, we give thanks for the
Commonwealth family of nations and pray that through the
relationships it fosters there may be brought about greater peace,
greater prosperity and greater integrity in our world.

God of all the earth,
in the life and teaching of your Son
you hold before us the vision of a world at peace, united as
    one family.
Strengthen the work of the Commonwealth,
that through political negotiations and practical projects
we may bring your vision closer to realization,
that the poor may be sustained,
the hungry fed
and the oppressed set free,
all for the sake of your Son,
Jesus Christ our Lord.

Leaders of the Nations

International Leaders

Leaders – integrity

O God of the whole world, we pray for the leaders of the nations and all in authority, that they may have honesty and integrity in their public life, that they may have the strength to advocate what is right even when it is unpopular, and that they may seek the peace of the whole world and equality and justice in their own societies.

God of all,
you alone can bring peace between nations and peace in our hearts.
Grant to our leaders such a longing for that peace,
that they may seek it above all human gain of money, glory
    or power.
May they hold always in their minds the needs of those
    they govern,
may they have compassion on those in distress
and through their actions may more and more of the peoples of
    the world
be brought to flourishing and joy in this life,
through Jesus Christ our Lord.

Leaders – integrity and civility

Lord, we pray for your world. We pray for our leaders, that they
may govern with wisdom and with commitment to the common
good, and we pray for all political discourse, that it would
be filled with reason, understanding and respect rather than
negativity, anger and violence.

God of all,
in whose stillness is the essence of perfect wisdom
and in whose love is the fulfilment of perfect care,
pour out your Spirit of grace on all those who lead our nation
in politics, in the media and in civil society.
Teach them to eschew personal and party advantage in the quest
    for the common good,
strengthen them to condemn aggression and falsehood
even when it seems to serve their purposes,
and encourage within them
all that is discerning, principled and hopeful,
that, together with them,
we may inherit a future of prosperity, justice and peace
    throughout our world,
through Jesus Christ our Lord.

Leaders – Spirit of wisdom and understanding, Spirit of counsel and might

Generous God, pour out on our leaders your Holy Spirit, we
pray, that guided by you in all things they would build the world
for which you long.

God of all,
whose unity of love is our eternal goal,
breathe on our leaders your Holy Spirit,
the Spirit of wisdom and understanding,
the Spirit of counsel and might,
the Spirit of knowledge and the fear of the Lord,
that through reaching out to one another in heart and mind,
they may direct our steps in the paths of peace, justice and hope,
through Jesus Christ our Lord.

Leaders – working for peace

Lord, we pray for all who are in positions of authority in this
and every land, and for a strengthening among all people of our
commitment to walk together the pilgrimage of life in fellowship
with those of all backgrounds, cultures and traditions.

God of all the earth,
you created all people in a rich diversity
and you show each of us something of the meaning of your
    creation and love.
Strengthen our leaders in the knowledge of your will,
that they may lead us all in the paths of peace,
and show us how to join together in our human journey,
not as rivals or as competitors but as one family,
through one who calls us not servants but friends,
even Jesus Christ our Lord.

Leaders – look to the needs of those they serve

Lord, we pray for your world. We pray in particular at this time
for the leaders of the nations, that they would live up to the
great responsibilities with which they have been charged, that
they would pursue kindness to one another and to those they
serve, and that through their insight and their relationships, the
whole world would be led towards a future of greater equality,
prosperity and unity.

Heavenly Father,
whose Son Jesus Christ came not to be served but to serve,
pour into the hearts of our leaders that same spirit of service,
that in all they say and in all they do
they may look to the needs of those who have the least,
and through wisdom and honesty
speak out for a world where fairness, friendship and
    integrity reign,
through Jesus Christ our Lord.

Leaders – servant-leadership

Lord, we pray for your world, for openness and fairness on the
part of all leaders, and for a renewed commitment, from all those
whose decisions affect the lives of others, to look to the needs of
those they serve before their own advantage.

Loving God,
whose Son came among us as one who serves,
teach our hearts to love the service of others.
Keep us all from the temptations of selfishness and love of power,
and, in humility, inspire us to wash one another's feet,
that as we offer them love and care
we may know that in the least of them
we are ministering to your Son,
in whose service is our perfect freedom,
even Jesus Christ our Lord.

Leaders – grant them the virtues of a true leader
(Christ the King)

Lord, [as we celebrate our eternal King,] we pray for all those
who exercise leadership in this world.

Almighty God,
whose Son Jesus Christ calls us not servants but friends,
and came not to be served but to serve,
grant his spirit of humility to all those who lead the nations of this
    earth.
Take from them all pride and love of personal gain,
and grant them
judgement in confusion,
courage in adversity
and compassion in all things,
that through their actions
our world may be a place of greater fairness, respect and
    enjoyment for all peoples,
through the transforming power of the King of Glory,
Jesus Christ our Lord.

Leaders – working for peace, not self-interest

Lord, we pray for your world, for the leaders of the nations, that they would seek what unites and not what divides, for the work of the United Nations and all international agencies, and for each one of us, that we may build communities where justice and peace are at home.

God of peace,
guide with your wisdom all those who lead our world.
Show them your justice,
that they may pursue that peace which is grounded in true
    freedom and equality
and may turn away from the temptation to rule through fear.
Show them your love,
that they may work together for the good of all those they serve
and leave behind selfishness and indifference to the welfare
    of others.
Show them your hope,
that they may have the courage to imagine a future transformed
    by your love
and the commitment to work towards it in all their decisions day
    by day,
through Jesus Christ our Lord.

Leaders – working for unity

Lord, we pray for your world and especially for our leaders, that following the example of your Son they would know that true glory comes not through power or superiority but through the gifts of love and service, and that considering the needs of others before their own, they would seek always that peace which brings about flourishing and happiness for all humanity.

King of peace,
you created the earth in harmony
and in all our moments of discord you call us back to harmony
    once again.
Breathe on the leaders of the nations your Spirit of peace,
that leaving aside all pride, ambition and hatred
they would seek the unity and tranquillity of the whole world,
and lead us, your people, in ways of friendship, understanding
    and love,
that the wounds of humanity would be healed
and our voices would be joined together as one,
in Jesus Christ our Lord.

Leaders – working for unity by God's grace

Lord, we pray for your world. We pray for all those taking crucial decisions about our shared future, for a spirit of wisdom and judgement, for a spirit of restraint and self-control, for a spirit of cooperation and openness to others' views, that we may be enabled by your grace to heal our divisions and live generously and creatively with our differences.

God of love,
in whose Son all the contradictions of humanity are overcome
and all the strife of this world is transformed into heaven's
    perfect peace,
shed on our leaders this day the light of your guidance,
that turning to seek your wisdom in the quietness of their hearts
they may be granted the insight to know what is best
and the courage to pursue it,
through Jesus Christ our Lord.

Leaders – a time of difficulty

Lord, we pray for your world. In this time of uncertainty we pray
for our leaders, for our communities and all those for whom we
are particularly anxious at this time.

God of truth,
by whose wisdom all good counsel, all just judgement and all
    right decisions flow,
pour out your Spirit of wisdom on our leaders.
In their planning and decision-making give them insight and
    understanding,
in their communications with us grant them honesty
    and compassion.
Bless all who suffer with your comfort,
strengthen all who are weak with your power,
calm all who are anxious with your peace
and help us as a nation, and as an international community,
to work together and support one another
in moments of strength and in moments of difficulty,
through Jesus Christ our Lord.

Leaders – a time of hope

Lord of hope, we pray for all who are entrusted with the
leadership of others. As we hear of hopeful signs of progress
in our world, we pray that these fragile possibilities may take
root and grow in strength. We pray for better futures for all
the peoples of the world, for integrity in public life and for the
wisdom and intelligence among our leaders to find just solutions
to the most taxing and complex of situations.

Lord of life,
you strengthen all that is good
and give good heart to those who do right in their purposes.
Be with the leaders of the world we pray,
that through your guidance
they may discern what is best for their people,
and through your power
they may have the resolve and the support to fulfil it,
through Jesus Christ our Lord.

Leaders of this Nation

Leaders of this nation – our Queen (on her birthday)

Lord, we pray for our world. [On this her birthday] we give
thanks for the life and dedication of our Queen, praying for her
continued good health and strength in the many responsibilities
that are laid on her. At this time, we pray in particular for her
leadership of the Commonwealth and for the flourishing of
that family of nations in our work towards a fairer and more
prosperous future.

King of kings and Lord of lords,
in whose hands are the destinies of nations
and under whose direction alone justice, peace and good will
    can thrive,
bless this day Elizabeth our Queen,
guide and strengthen her in her life of service
and help her to find satisfaction in all she has achieved,
that she and all we who are her subjects
may live in the confidence of your abiding love and aid,
through Jesus Christ our Lord.

Leaders of this nation – strength, duty and compassion

King of kings, we pray for all those working in national and local
government. We give you thanks for their commitment to the
people of this country, their willingness to serve even in the face
of cynicism and hostility, and for the energy they give to national
and local affairs. We pray that they may discharge their office
with integrity, that they may always be mindful of the needs of
those whose voices may not be the loudest, and that many people
of ability and compassion would be inspired to offer themselves
for such public service.

Lord of all,
who has taught us that true judgement is only exercised in love
and that true authority is only held in service,
bless, we pray, all those who have the responsibilities of
    government in this land.
When they grow weary, strengthen and refresh them,
when they are uncertain, give them your humility and
    your wisdom,
when they are tempted to put their own concerns before those of
    the people they serve,
remind them of their duty to their common life,
that through their initiatives, their sound management and their
    fruitful debates,
we may live together in unity, peace and happiness,
through Jesus Christ our Lord.

Leaders of this nation – servant-leadership

We pray for our Queen, giving thanks for her long and self-giving
ministry to this nation, and praying for her continued strength
and well-being. We pray too for our political leaders, that they
may know that greatness is found most profoundly in the gift of
service to others.

Lord God,
we thank you that your Son Jesus Christ came among us as one
    who serves,
and that through his actions and his words we have been taught a
    nobler way to lead.
Grant your wisdom to all in places of authority in this and
    every land,
that they may know your will
and, keeping always before their minds the needs of others,
may discover that in serving them they are serving you,
through the same Jesus Christ our Lord.

Leaders of this nation – the courage to distinguish between the popular and the right

Lord of lords, we pray for all who offer themselves to take on positions of leadership in our public life, for our politicians and our judges, for our civil servants and our community leaders. In times of great cynicism, we give thanks for the sacrifices they make to serve us, and pray that they would discharge their office with integrity, wisdom and compassion.

Lord of all,
your Son taught us that anyone who would be first must
    become last
and be the true servant of all.
Grant to those who lead our nation and local communities that
    spirit of service,
that following the example of your Son
they may have the courage to distinguish between what is popular
    and what is right,
the openness to learn from the ideas and policies of others
and the compassion to seek, most of all, to serve those who have
    the least,
through Jesus Christ our Lord.

Leaders of this nation – wisdom and justice

King of kings, we pray for all those who are entrusted with positions of leadership in this and every land, for our Queen and her government, for all who serve in local councils and for all in authority, that they may be enriched with understanding and compassion in all that they do on our behalf.

Lord of the whole world,
in the life of your Son you have shown us
that all true authority is lived out in service.
Inspire all who lead in our nation,
that they may look not to personal advantage
but to the common good,
and grant them space in their work to reflect and to rest,
that freed from the chaos of instant reactions
they may be guided by the wisdom that comes from you alone,
in your Son, Jesus Christ our Lord.

Leaders of this nation – your spirit of wisdom and unity

Father of all peoples, we pray for the life of our nation, for
our Queen and all those in authority under her, for our Prime
Minister and the government, for all Members of Parliament, for
all working in local government, for judges and for all those with
responsibility for our common life.

Lord, through whose wisdom the universe was formed in
   the beginning
and is held in being in its every moment,
grant to those who lead our nation that same spirit of wisdom,
that they may listen with carefulness,
decide with understanding
and live with integrity,
that the people of this land may grow together in unity,
in mutual understanding
and in charity to the world,
through Jesus Christ our Lord.

Political Life

Elections

An election

We pray today [for our nation, and especially for today's
election,] for all who are standing for elected office, for all who
will vote, for a full and constructive engagement in the democratic
process and for a spirit of social harmony and seeking the
common good, whatever the result.

Heavenly Father,
we give you thanks for the blessings of the freedom we enjoy.
Help each one of us to play our part in our political life
with thoughtfulness, sound judgement and respect for the
    perspectives of others.
Grant to us all, at this time, your Spirit of wisdom,
that we may cast our votes in hope and confidence
and work in this world for the coming of your kingdom,
through Jesus Christ our Lord.

An election in a troubled place

Lord, we pray for your world, and in particular for the people of
N as they vote in their election, that the voting in that place may
be conducted in security and with fairness, and that the public life
of all nations would be characterized by integrity and common
purpose in pursuit of the good of all.

God of all nations,
whose longing is for all peoples to be free,
be with all those who cast their vote today in N and throughout
    our world.
May their elections be free and fair,
may their leaders act with integrity and justice
and may their future be filled with hope and promise
as they exercise their democratic rights,
through Jesus Christ our Lord.

An election – those standing for office

Lord our guide, we pray for all those standing for elected office
in this country at this time, that they would campaign with
openness, honesty and respect for others.

Heavenly Father,
we thank you for the political freedoms and rights that we enjoy
    in this land,
and for the commitment of those who offer themselves for
    public office.
Direct the hearts of all those who seek election at this time,
that they may speak with integrity, wisdom and compassion,
and help all who vote to have a true sense of our responsibilities,
and sound judgement as we make our decision,
through Jesus Christ our Lord.

An election – voters and government in this land

Lord, as we thank you for the freedoms we enjoy in our country,
so we pray for our national life, asking that you would bless both
those in government and each one of us, as together we work for
a better future for this land and for our world.

Lord our God,
guide the leaders of our land,
that they may show integrity in their public life,
wisdom in their decision-making,
compassion in their speaking,
and courage in times of difficulty,
and strengthen all the members of our society,
that we may shun the temptations of cynicism and conflict,
and work together to bring about
the relief of suffering,
the increase of opportunity,
the peace of all nations,
and the nurture of our environment,
through Jesus Christ our Lord.

Politicians

Politicians – working for the common good

Lord of all, we pray for the leaders of this country, for
the government and for the opposition, and for a spirit of
constructive dialogue and discernment about the way ahead for
our land. We pray also today for any who are feeling alienated
or unrepresented by our political system, and for a greater sense
of connection between politicians and people and between our
different communities.

Lord of the nations,
grant your wisdom to all those in authority
and give them your courage to apply that wisdom with integrity,
with clarity of purpose
and with compassion.
Let not the extremes of party politics or posturing blind those
    who govern
or motivate those who oppose,
so that we may all honour one another
and seek only the common good,
through Jesus Christ our Lord

Politicians – political parties

Lord, we pray for your world. We pray for all political parties, for
their role in bringing together the views of many individuals and
working to articulate a common purpose, for their openness and
integrity and for their commitment to the good of the nations they
seek to serve.

God of all,
we give you thanks for the power of dialogue to bring
    people together,
for the gift of compromise
and for the possibilities opened to us by shared purpose.
Bless all those who are members of political parties,
that lifting their eyes beyond internal dispute and
    sectarian advantage
they may come together to articulate a future for our world
that is filled with hope, justice, fairness and respect for the
    rights of all,
through Jesus Christ our Lord.

Politicians & opinion formers – may they seek the common good

Lord we pray for your world. We pray for all politicians, for those who work in the media and for all who shape our political discourse and national life. We pray for a renewed civility in discussions, for a deeper willingness to find practical compromises and for inspiration and vision in approaching the future with wisdom and hope.

God of all,
in whose wisdom is the path of peace
and through whose guidance all right decisions are made,
be with those who lead our world at this difficult and
    uncertain time.
Strengthen their insight into what is best for the people
and give them courage to pursue the common good,
that, laying aside personal or party advantage, they may argue for
    a future
that will bring about the flourishing of all nations
and the greater peace and prosperity of our world,
through Jesus Christ our Lord.

The Rule of Law & the Administration of Justice

The Rule of Law

Rule of law – places of lawlessness

Loving God, we thank you for the safety and security we enjoy in this land, and for all those police and others who put themselves at risk to defend the everyday business of life. We pray for all those places in the world where there is no security, for those who live in a land that is not their own, for those who are marginalized or persecuted by the authorities, and for those who live in daily fear of war or terrorism.

Heavenly Father,
as once you brought your chosen people to a place of safety
where they could rest from all those who oppressed them,
so this day, we pray, bring security and comfort to all those who
   live in danger.
Bring stability to places of lawlessness,
unity to places of division
and justice to places of oppression,
so that through the whole world we may see made manifest
that peace and fellowship of all humanity,
for which your Son laid down his life,
even Jesus Christ our Lord.

Rule of law – places of lawlessness and those who suffer there

Lord, we pray for your world and especially for all places of violence and danger. We pray for communities marked by the ravages of war and terrorism, places of lawlessness and cruelty and places of poverty and hunger. As we ask each day for the coming of your kingdom, we hold in prayer our longing for a transformation of all those places, that they may become like that kingdom of justice and peace which is the kingdom of your Son.

Lord of all,
you created us for joy
and yet so many live in misery,
you created us for fellowship
and yet so many live in hostility.
Be, this day, in all those places of hurt and anguish in the world,
dry the tears of the weeping,
give new hope to the desolate,
renew with inspiration and energy all who work for change,
that the whole earth would be filled with the people you long for:
human beings, fully alive,
through Jesus Christ our Lord.

The Administration of Justice

Justice – the administration of justice

Lord, we pray for our world, for all those who serve us in public life and especially for all those involved in the administration of justice. We pray for the police, for prison and probation officers, for lawyers and legal advisors and for all judges, that they may fulfil their vocations with integrity and impartiality, with wisdom and with compassion for all.

Lord God,
judge of all the earth,
we pray that your justice may be known in this and every land.
Take from our world the scourge of dishonesty,
the cruelty of corruption
and the brutality of violence,
and grant to all those who enforce the law on our behalf
uprightness in their actions,
shrewdness in their deliberations
and fairness in their decisions,
through one who knew himself the cost of injustice,
even Jesus Christ our Lord.

Justice – false accusations

Lord, we pray for all who are victims of false accusations,
for those who do not have a proper opportunity to defend
themselves, for all who suffer because of dishonesty or oversights
among police and prosecutors, for those who live in places where
justice is not administered in a fair way, and for all who work to
bring fairness and justice to our world.

God of justice,
guardian of truth,
defender of the oppressed,
bring your justice to our world.
Where there is corruption, bring your purity,
where there is negligence, bring your care,
where there is unfairness, bring your equality,
that right would triumph
and falsehood fail,
through Jesus Christ our Lord.

Justice – judges

Heavenly Father, we pray for all members of the judiciary in this and every land. We pray that they may exercise authority with integrity, understanding and fairness, and we pray for all those places where judges are corrupt or in league with oppressive governments, that they may recover all justice and the rule of law.

O God of truth,
strengthen with your wisdom
all those who serve as judges in this and every land.
Grant them discernment in their work
and fairness in their judgments,
that both strong and weak may be treated with equity,
through Jesus Christ our Lord.

Justice – gift of the law (Advent: O Adonai)

Lord, who gave the law on Sinai, we pray for all those who fashion our laws today, for the government of this and every nation, for our judges and police and for all those responsible for enforcing the law, for all who serve as jurors and especially for all those who live under unjust regimes or in places where the rule of law has broken down, that you, Lord, would come and redeem them with an outstretched arm.

Almighty God,
we give you thanks that you are a God who loves justice.
Bring your justice, we pray, to this and every land.
Direct the counsels and desires of those in authority,
encourage and protect all those working in law enforcement
and grant wisdom and integrity to all who sit in judgement,
that your will may be done in our society and throughout
    our world,
through Jesus Christ our Lord.

Justice – prisoners (Advent: O Clavis David)

Lord Jesus Christ, who has come to lead the prisoners from the prison house, we pray for all who are imprisoned this day. We pray for those justly imprisoned, that they may find rehabilitation and restoration, and for prisoners of conscience and all who are oppressed, that you would bring them to the freedom for which they long.

Christ our Light,
you are coming to bring your hope to all those who dwell in the
    darkness of despair.
Enlighten, we pray, with your truth
all those detained in prison and all those who detain them,
that the guilty may know penitence and begin a journey
    of restoration,
that the innocent would be freed
and that the oppressors would learn to follow the paths of justice,
that the whole world would come to know
the brightness of your shining
and the glory of your kingdom,
where you live and reign with the Father and the Holy Spirit,
one God, now and for ever.

Social Justice

Social justice – work for fairness

Lord, we pray for your world and especially for those most in need. As we worship in this place of safety and beauty, we pray for all who are homeless this day, all those without work and all those who go hungry. We pray for all charities, food banks and shelters, we pray for all those who advise and guide others and we pray for all in authority, that the needs of those who have least may be a constant concern in all their policy-making and government.

Lord of all,
whose only Son became poor so that we might become rich,
and entered into this world without shelter in a land under foreign
    occupation,
we pray for all those in need this day,
that they would find good helpers to sustain them in all that they do.
Strengthen all who work for fairness in this and every land,
that through their work the lives of others would be improved
and all people would glimpse the purpose for which you made us:
to love and serve one another in Jesus Christ our Lord.

Social justice – a fairer world (Christ the King)

King of kings, we pray for your world, torn apart by the pride and acquisitiveness of the powerful. Bring peace and healing to all places of division, and grant relief to all those in distress. We pray especially today for those who so often suffer the consequences of others' actions: the poorest of our world. We pray for the hungry, the thirsty, the sick, the poor and the unemployed, that they may find respite and peace.

Lord of all,
transform the life of the kingdoms of this world
to be like unto the kingdom of your Son.
Bring about, we pray, in our world and through our actions,
fairer economic systems,
that the hungry may be fed,
fairer educational systems,
that all may find work suited to their talents,
and fairer political systems,
that the oppressed may speak freely,
through the power of one who was the victim of this
    world's injustice
but now reigns in heaven as its king,
even Jesus Christ our Lord.

Social justice – sharing what we have

Lord, we pray for your world. We pray for those who work
to reduce inequalities and injustices in society, for the work of
charities who support the poorest in our world, for those who
give up their own time as private individuals to serve those in
need, and for all those who receive their care.

Lord Jesus Christ,
you taught us that you are known most profoundly
among those who have the least,
and that the poor are blessed indeed.
May we who enjoy so much plenty
be inspired by your call, echoed through the centuries by
    your Saints,
to share what we have with others,
that all might have enough
to enjoy the life that is the free gift of God,
Father, Son and Holy Spirit.

Oppression

Oppression (Advent: O Radix Jesse)

Lord God, whose Son came to set us free, we pray for all those in need of your powerful deliverance this day. We pray for all those who live in places of oppression, those who suffer because of the unfair structures and practices of our own society, and for all who are enslaved to addictions and unhealthy patterns of behaviour that seem beyond their control.

Lord of power,
your Son Jesus Christ came to deliver us from all that keeps us
    from the fullness of life.
Be with each person who, this day,
has their life diminished by the impositions of others
or by the cruelty of compulsions that have clouded their joy.
May the coming among us of your Son be to them a sign of
the hope of healing,
the hope of deliverance
and the hope of a life given new purpose and meaning,
in the passion and Resurrection of Jesus Christ our Lord.

Oppression – those who speak out (John the Baptist)

Lord, we pray for your world. [As we recall John the Baptist's brave speaking of the truth, in the face of the violence of others, so] we pray for all who speak truth to power in our own day, giving thanks for their courage and their clear-sightedness, and praying for their protection from all who would use force to silence them.

God of truth,
again and again you have raised up prophets to speak the truth of
    your love
when cruelty was convenient,
and to speak of peace and justice
when human beings preferred expansion and greed.
Be with all those who speak out as prophets in our own day,
guide their pronouncements with your wisdom and compassion
and grant us the insight to know what word truly comes from you,
and the humility to take it to heart and put it into action,
through Jesus Christ our Lord.

Oppression – persecution on the grounds of political belief

We pray for all who are persecuted in our time for their faith or
political beliefs, for all those falsely imprisoned, tortured or living
in fear of being discovered, for the work of Amnesty International
and for all who build up freedom of belief and expression
throughout the world.

Lord, you have taught us that the truth will set us free.
Bring your wisdom to all seekers of truth,
giving them courage to follow where their investigations lead
and steadfastness in their witness to what is right.
Be with all those who dare to speak out in places where the truth
    is dangerous,
and grant your strength to all those who work to give a voice
to those whose voices others would wish to silence,
that we may become a world that yearns to listen more, learn
    more and judge less,
through Jesus Christ our Lord.

Oppression – freedom and justice everywhere

Lord God, we pray for your world. We pray for an end to
political violence of any kind. We pray that all societies
would tolerate open debate and questioning, for an end to the
imprisonment and torture of political rivals and for a renewed
focus throughout the international community on the dignity and
rights of individuals, whatever the political consequences.

God of kindness and truth,
in you we live, move and have our being.
Reveal to the eyes of all the surpassing worth of every human being.
Deliver the oppressed from their persecutors,
set free those falsely imprisoned
and keep us as individuals and as a society
from the temptations of not wanting to see or speak or act,
that empowered by your Spirit
and fired by your love,
we would not rest content until the justice and freedom that
    we enjoy
becomes the common possession of all,
through Jesus Christ our Lord.

Oppression – freedom rather than fear

Lord, we pray for a commitment to open government and
freedom throughout our world.

God of justice,
whose longing is for all people to find fulfilment in community,
guide our leaders,
that the shape of our societies may serve the flourishing of all.
Take from the powerful the desire to use fear as a mechanism
    of control,
and from the international community
the desire to prioritize our prosperity over the pursuit of right,
that all peoples may come to know
that the best hope of peace and stability lies in freedom,
and the best source of productivity lies in communities open
    to change,
through one who came to make all things new,
even Jesus Christ our Lord.

Oppression – victims of oppression

Lord, we pray for your world, and we remember especially before
you today those places that are deprived of the freedoms we enjoy
here. We pray for a respect for human dignity throughout the
earth, for an end to discrimination and prejudice, and for freedom
of conscience for all people.

God of justice,
you hear the cry of the imprisoned
and the anguish of the oppressed.
In your mercy, bring deliverance, we pray,
to all those places labouring under brutal governments or criminal
    control.
Grant, to all those who suffer, the comfort of your Spirit
and the hope of a future transformed by your love,
that working together with our brothers and sisters throughout
    the world
we may begin to craft a humanity more worthy of its creator,
in Jesus Christ our Lord.

Oppression – perpetrators of oppression

Lord, we pray for your world. We pray for a greater respect throughout our world for human rights, for an end to the use of judicial violence and discrimination to secure popular approval, and for positive action on the part of the international community to promote the well-being and freedom of all people.

God our Father,
protect from harm all those you have created and called your
    beloved children.
Take from those in authority the temptation to inflict suffering on
    others
to win approval for themselves,
and take from us all the apathy and selfishness
that leads us to ignore the sufferings of the weak,
that through working together, and standing up for the truth,
we may leave to our children
a world of equality, freedom and peace,
through Jesus Christ our Lord.

Oppression – may the leaders of the nations work for a better world

God of compassion, we pray for your world, for all places of violence and instability, where cruelty goes unnoticed and where crime goes unpunished. We pray for the leaders of the nations, that they would work to bring reconciliation and unity within their own countries, and together work for a more just and peaceful world.

God of all nations,
your wisdom is greater than human intelligence
and your power is greater than human strength.
Bring about, we pray, your kingdom in this our suffering world.
Protect the oppressed,
reconcile the divided,
heal the hurting
and guide our leaders in paths of justice and peace,
that the whole world may reflect the love and the unity of
    its creator,
through Jesus Christ our Lord.

Oppression – those who work to combat oppression (William Wilberforce, Olaudah Equiano & Thomas Clarkson)

Lord, we pray for your Church. [On this day when we remember William Wilberforce, Olaudah Equiano, Thomas Clarkson and all those who campaigned for the abolition of slavery,] we pray for those who work to set all people free in body, mind and spirit.

God of all,
whose Son taught us that the truth shall set us free,
so deepen our spirits in the truth of the faith
that our souls, set free from the chains of prejudice and cruelty,
would be filled with hope and purpose,
that we would dedicate our lives
to comforting those weighed down by suffering,
defending those crushed by oppression
and challenging those who persecute others,
for the sake of one who called us not servants but friends,
even Jesus Christ our Lord.

Oppression – modern slavery and forced labour (William Wilberforce, Olaudah Equiano & Thomas Clarkson)

Lord, we pray for your world. [As we give thanks for the abolitionist movement,] we pray for all those who continue to be afflicted by the evil of slavery today, for all victims of modern slavery and human trafficking, for all those who work for poverty-wages or under cruel management, for those who are employed illegally without the rights and protections we enjoy.

God of justice,
who in the wonderful gift of creation showed us work's potential,
and in Christ's labour as a craftsman showed us work's dignity,
protect all those forced to work this day against their will.
Deliver those whose dignity is ignored or attacked
from those who abuse them for their own purposes.
Strengthen those who work for justice for all
and protect all those who live in danger,
that all peoples would be enabled to use their creativity in freedom
to sustain their lives
and enrich their souls,
through Jesus Christ our Lord.

Violence

Violence – take away our will for violence

Father of all peoples, in a world divided by violence and prejudice
we pray for the gift of your reconciling love, for greater respect
between those of different faiths and political views, and for those
whose lives have been torn apart by works of hate.

Lord God, through your Son Jesus Christ
you made peace between the different peoples of this world.
Take from us all cruelty towards one another,
all prejudice, all apathy, all desire to overpower and control,
and fill our hearts with your love,
that we may see in one another the image of your glory,
and that through serving others
we may come to imitate the one who came not to be served but
    to serve,
even Jesus Christ our Lord.

Violence – Christ a victim of violence

Lord, we pray for all those whose lives have been affected by
the violence of others throughout our world, for all those who
have lost their lives, for those with permanent injuries, for those
suffering with mental trauma and for all those who have lost
loved ones or who continue to suffer with them. Grant, we pray,
to those who died in violence the peace of your eternal kingdom,
and to those who live on, the healing and comfort of your
Holy Spirit.

O God,
whose Son Jesus Christ
came among us in the vulnerability of a newborn child
and suffered the violence of humanity on the Cross,
that your power might be known most perfectly in weakness,
we hold before you this day
those whom the brutality of others has harmed
and all those who live in the daily fear of the cruelty of
     the powerful.
Be a shield round about them, O God, we pray,
and teach us all gentleness,
that through cherishing the surpassing worth of each human life
we may do honour to the word made flesh among us,
even Jesus Christ our Lord.

Violence – extremism and lack of respect for others

We pray for an end to violent extremism, for a changing of heart
of those who would seek to impose their will on others through
cruelty, for renewed respect for every individual, no matter their
religion, gender or sexuality. We pray for fresh hope in places of
devastation, for the sense that a future of peace might be viable,
and for a working-together and fellowship that would prevent a
return to the rule of force.

Lord of all peoples,
you love us all with one equal love.
Help us in our human frailty to avoid the temptation to
   dominate others
to feel secure ourselves.
Grant us your gift of compassion, we pray,
that through serving others we may discover our true identity,
our true dignity and our true worth,
through the power of one who emptied himself to be with us in all
   things,
even Jesus Christ our Lord.

Violence – the cost of human freedom

Lord, we pray for your peace amid the pain of this world. As
we give thanks for the freedom of action you have granted us,
we acknowledge its cost and we pray for all those who suffer as
victims of others' cruelty.

Father of us all,
you rule over all things yet you come to us in gentleness;
you direct the course of history yet you promise never to take
   away our freedom.
Be with those who suffer the consequences of the human capacity
   for cruelty
and lust for control.
Bring your peace, this night, to all those who suffer the violence of
   others,
peace to wounded bodies,
peace to wounded hearts,
peace to wounded communities
and peace to a wounded world,
that learning from our sufferings
we would build a world in which all can thrive,
through Jesus Christ our Lord.

Violence – knife/gun crime

Lord, we pray for your world. As our media reflect on a surge in the number of violent attacks in our country, we pray for an end to violence on our streets and for the safety and nurturing of our young people. We pray for those who, through fear and pride, feel the need to carry weapons and to threaten or hurt others, that they would find more stable and productive ways to feel secure and valued. We pray for the police and others working to reduce violent crime, and for all those whose work is to raise the aspirations and to nurture the social responsibility of the young people of our cities.

God our Father,
you hold all of your children in one equal love.
Protect those, we pray, who live at the risk of violence.
Take from our streets the weapons that cause so much harm,
take from the hearts of our people the brutality and insecurity
that lead them to mistreat others,
and strengthen all those who work for good in our communities,
that through cooperation and commitment
we may bring about a future full of hope and purpose for all,
through Jesus Christ our Lord.

Violence – perpetrators of violence
(Conversion of St Paul)

Lord, we pray for your world. [As we remember this day the conversion of Paul, so] we pray for all those intent on violence, cruelty and destruction, that their hearts would be changed and their lives transformed. We pray for all perpetrators of unjust warfare, criminality, bullying and aggression, and for all of those whose lives are blighted by their actions.

Lord God,
whose human creation has such a capacity to hurt as well as
    to heal,
breathe your transforming Spirit afresh on all who intend to
    do evil.
Open their eyes to the harm their actions cause to others,
open their hearts to feel compassion for those they attack,
and teach them to leave behind selfishness, pride and arrogance,
and learn a new love for the just, the gentle and the true,
through Jesus Christ our Lord.

Violence – terrorism – teach us the priority of peace

God of peace, we pray today for all those tempted to use violence
to achieve their ends, for those in danger of manipulation into
terrorist action, and for the commitment of us all to finding safe
ways to hear the voices of those who feel disenfranchised, and to
resolving disputes through negotiation.

God of compassion,
you call us to dwell together in unity
and to enjoy the journey of life in the enriching company of others.
Show to us all the priority of peace.
Take from jealous and frustrated hearts the desire to use violence
    to get their way,
and teach us to pursue loving and honest ways of resolving
    our differences,
that through openness of mind and a longing to listen,
we may find ways of being together that serve the good of all,
through Jesus Christ our Lord.

Violence – victims of violence

Lord, we pray for your world, for all places where war and
violence are everyday realities. We pray for those who fear the
onslaught of enemies they cannot escape or control, for an end
to the pride and acquisitiveness that lead us to hurt one another
in selfishness, and for wisdom to resolve more peaceably our
differences and divisions.

God of power,
stretch out your right hand, we pray,
to defend those who are the victims of others' violence,
and give strength to those who fear violence that is to come.
Show to the desperate your wisdom,
to the terrified your hope
and to the cruel your compassion and your justice,
that together we may work for a world of peace and righteousness,
a place where joy and contentment may be found in life,
and understanding and friendship would be known
    between communities,
through Jesus Christ our Lord.

Challenging Times

A Time of Fear

A time of fear – help us to trust in you

Lord, in this difficult time, help us to know your peace, that we
may react to all that is happening in our world with calmness and
with wisdom.

Lord, you have taught us that perfect love casts out fear,
and yet the news we hear every day gives us cause to be alarmed.
Help us all, in our weakness and fragility,
to entrust our lives to your care,
and share with us the burden of our anxieties,
that we may experience the joy of that fullness of life
for which we have been created, redeemed and sanctified,
in Jesus Christ our Lord.

A time of fear – let us know your peace

God of peace, in whom alone is our trust and our confidence,
strengthen our hearts at this time of fear, that through knowing
your presence with us we would be enabled to live with generosity
and compassion.

Lord God,
your reign is over all the earth
and your kingdom knows no end.
Be with all your faithful people in times of fear and danger,
that we may find in you
the warmth of comfort,
the light of hope
and the stillness of peace,
in Jesus Christ our Lord.

A Time of Transition

Nations in a time of transition

Lord, we pray for your world and for all nations and individuals
going through testing times of change and transformation, that, in
hope, a future of new possibilities would open up for them.

God of all the world,
whose Son came to make all things new,
we give you thanks for the changing seasons of life
and for the breaking forth of your new creation each day.
Be with those nations and people
whose lives change radically this day,
that through knowing your companionship with them on
    the journey,
they may walk onwards with confidence, expectation
    and creativity,
through Jesus Christ our Lord.

Our Nation

*Our nation – its government and its divisions
(a national patron saint)*

Lord, [on this day when we celebrate N the patron of this land,]
we pray for the life of our nation, for wisdom and integrity in
government, for reconciliation among our people, for a renewed
determination to work for the harmony of our communities,
and for fresh hope for the future and a renewed commitment to
mutual service.

Creator of all,
at the very beginnings of humanity you recognized that it was not
    good for us to be alone,
and you call us again and again
to seek our fulfilment and our identity in a life that is shared.
Refresh with your heavenly grace the peoples of this land,
that we may learn to serve one another,
to love our neighbours as ourselves
and to be people of peace and ambassadors of reconciliation in
    our communities,
so that we may discover once again how good and pleasant it is
for sisters and brothers to dwell together in unity,
through Jesus Christ our Lord.

Our nation – leadership in a time of difficulty

Lord, we pray for your world. In difficult and uncertain times
for our nation, we pray for our leaders and for all those who in
small and great ways work for the cause of unity and peace in our
community.

God our Father,
whose longing is for us to live in peace with one another, and in
    hope for a better future,
show your mercy to a land so much in need.
Guide our leaders with your wisdom,
strengthen our people with your compassion and commitment
and show us all that path ahead which leads to you,
that we may move from conflict and aggression
to understanding and renewal,
through Jesus Christ our Lord.

Local Community

Local community – our community

Heavenly Father, we pray for our local community and its needs.
We pray for all those who live and work here, for any who are
struggling at this time, for all who are looking for work but have
not yet found it, for those who live in poverty or on the streets
or alone. We pray that every person in this community would
know your love and your care for them, and that we would build
together ever stronger friendships with those with whom we share
our lives.

Look, we pray, O Lord,
on this our community.
Strengthen what is good within it
and teach us to cherish it.
Wherever there is suffering,
send your aid
and renew our commitment to one another,
that in our everyday lives
we may bear one another's burdens
and rejoice to share one another's joys,
through Jesus Christ our Lord.

Local community – the value of community

Lord, we pray for our city of N/for our county of N, giving thanks for the great richness of our shared life in this place. We pray for all who seek to serve the common good in their different areas of work, and for those who seek to offer their talents, in all their diversity, for the service of others.

Heavenly Father,
who has called each one of us to be in this place
and has made human community the context
in which we learn the meaning of friendship, joy and service,
strengthen all those who live and work in our city/county,
that the quality of our common life
may speak of the glorious potential of the human spirit
and the enjoyment that can be had when we engage fully with
  our world,
through Jesus Christ our Lord.

Local community – unity (Guy Fawkes Night)

Lord, we pray for your world. On this Guy Fawkes Night, with its memories of catastrophe averted but also its associations with religious strife and marginalization, we give thanks for the variety of faith and culture that we know in our national life. We pray for harmony between different communities, for respect for one another's traditions and dignity, for a commitment on the part of all to seek the common good, and for the courage to build up unity rather than to exploit division.

God of all peoples,
you have placed within each one of us some glimpse of your truth.
Help us all, who share in a common humanity,
to know the value our diversity can bring to the formation of
    our character
and to the universal quest for the good.
Help all those who live in this land
to be open to the needs and the insights of others,
that, reaching across all that can divide us,
we may be drawn together in mutual love and service,
knowing one another not as enemies or rivals but as friends,
through Jesus Christ our Lord.

Local community in a time of need

Lord God, we pray for our local community at this difficult time.
Strengthen us in our care for one another, that as we serve those
in need, so we may be built up as a stronger, more generous and
more loving community for the future.

Father of all,
you call us to be generous to one another
and to recognize in others' faces the true image of your Son.
Give us grace as individuals
and as a whole society,
that in this time of difficulty
we may minister friendship and support
to all those who are in need this day,
and that, through this service,
we may become the community you long for us to be,
through Jesus Christ our Lord.

Local community – city life (St Dominic)

[As we remember St Dominic's particular concern for ministry to
the growing cities of his age, so] we pray for city life today. We
pray especially for harmony between the different communities
that make up modern cities, and for all those working under
high pressure or stress, and we pray for all residents of our cities
who have the least, that they may find decent accommodation,
fulfilling work and supportive communities.

Lord of all,
in the Holy Scriptures human history begins in a garden
but ends in one eternal and glorious city.
We pray for all those who live in cities this day.
We pray that the diversity of city life may function as a benefit
    rather than a threat,
that the physical closeness of individuals
may be matched by a growing fellowship with one another,
that the wealth of the city would be used to make adequate provision
for those who have least
and that within the busyness of life
there may be space for reflection, restoration and the life of
    the Spirit,
through the power of the one who knew
that his own life had to find its fulfilment and its end in the city
    of Jerusalem,
even Jesus Christ our Lord.

Local community – guides and local historians

Lord, we pray for your world, and we pray especially today for guides and local historians. As we thank you for their knowledge and their skill in communicating effectively, we pray that they would continue to flourish and grow in their work, that others would be drawn into the excitement and wisdom of our shared history in this place, and that the guides would themselves find satisfaction and encouragement in their important work.

God our leader,
from whom all true guidance comes,
we thank you for all our teachers
and for all who have opened to us the truths of the past
and its lessons for our present day.
Be with all who guide others in this ancient city/town,
that through their ministry
all who visit this place may come to understand the people of
   history more profoundly
and to experience the humanity we share with them more intensely,
in Jesus Christ our Lord.

Charities

Charity – all those involved in charity

Lord God, we pray for your world. We give thanks for all those who take part in public life and put their varied talents at the service of others. We give thanks in particular today for all those involved in charitable work and for those whose efforts are not widely known or acknowledged, and we pray that, through their work, many would be enabled to lead more fulfilled lives, and that they themselves would find satisfaction in offering help to others.

Almighty God,
in the child Jesus we see the dignity of receiving care from others,
and in his adult life we see the grace found in serving those
     around us.
We give thanks for all those who are involved in our own day
in the giving and receiving of care,
praying that those in need would have the courage to seek the
     support they require
and that those who have money, time and skills to offer
would be generous in giving of what they have to strengthen those
     who struggle
and to serve the common good,
through Jesus Christ our Lord.

Charity – help us to serve (a particular charity/charities)

Lord, we pray for your world. As we give thanks for the
charitable work of N, we pray for their continued flourishing and
for all who are recipients of their aid.

Almighty God,
who has given us all that is good,
the treasure of this planet and the joy of human community,
help us to serve those less fortunate than ourselves,
looking not to our own reputation or advantage
but to the reality of their need,
that the whole world would be brought to that life of flourishing,
which is both your gift and your will for us,
in Jesus Christ our Lord.

Charities – integrity in operation

Lord, we pray for our world. We pray especially for all those
organizations that minister to the needs of others. We pray for
integrity in the aid sector, firm governance and a commitment to
transparency of operation, that those in need would be served and
those who minister to them would be fairly treated.

God, giver of all good things,
healer of the sick
and friend of the poor,
we pray for all those who dedicate their lives to the service of others
in this country and abroad.
Grant them compassion always to put the needs of those they
    serve first,
grant them honour to treat all they encounter with respect
and grant them wisdom as they order their institutional life
to bring hope, restoration and opportunity
to a world so much in need of their ministry,
through Jesus Christ our Lord.

Charity workers & benefactors – may they know the companionship of Christ

Lord God, we pray for our world and especially for all those within it who seek to do good in difficult times. We pray for those working in places of danger, for those giving generously of their own time and resources, and for all those who dedicate their lives for the good of others, that our future may be one of harmony, peace and joy.

God of love,
from whom all good things come,
inspire, we pray, with your Spirit
all those who seek to do your work in this world.
Make them know your accompanying presence in their actions,
help them to see the fruits of their labours
and grant them the grace to rest and care for themselves in their turn,
that through their efforts,
in ever greater numbers, people may come to know you
and join in your mission of love to your creation,
known to us in Jesus Christ our Lord.

Charity workers & emergency services – in winter

Lord, we pray for your world, for charity workers, the emergency services and for all who work to bring safety to those in need.

Loving God,
in the cold we feel more keenly our own need of shelter, comfort
and love.
Bless all those who work to minister your warmth to others in
these cold days.
Where they are tired, refresh them,
where they feel overlooked, show them how deeply you value them,
where they are lost and in need of love themselves, open your
heart to them,
that as they minister to us
so they also would be ministered to by your undying care,
through Jesus Christ our Lord.

Family Life & The Seasons of Life

Family Life

Family life – its joys and difficulties

Lord, on this day we pray that your love would be made known
in all families. We pray for a deepening and strengthening of
the bonds that hold family life together. We pray for all families
where those bonds have broken down completely, or where there
is tension or mistrust. We pray for all those agencies that seek to
support people facing difficulties in their relationships, for greater
respect for different forms of families, and greater openness and
honesty about the difficulties of life together.

Lord God,
at our creation you said that it is not good for us to be alone.
We thank you for the gift of relationship,
for the blessings of friends and family,
and we pray that we would have the wisdom and the steadfastness
to nurture all our relationships,
in good times and in bad.
When family life is difficult and relations are strained,
help us to know your presence with us,
that we may draw on the knowledge that we belong to your family
and find the wisdom and confidence that we need to be faithful
    to others
and faithful to ourselves,
through Jesus Christ our Lord.

Family life – those far from loved ones

Heavenly Father, bless with your comfort all those who miss family members far away today, that they would know the unity they share with them in your infinite love.

God our Father,
from whom every family on earth takes its name,
be with all those who are far from loved ones today.
Ease their anxiety,
soften their sadness,
deepen their gratitude for one another
and remind us all of your love,
from which neither height, nor depth nor any other creature can
    separate us,
in Jesus Christ our Lord.

Family life – our family members far away

Lord God, we pray for all members of our families living far away, that we may work diligently to keep up our contact with them and may look forward with expectation to seeing them again in person.

God of love,
in whom we are all united
and from whom we can never be parted,
strengthen all those far from loved ones this day.
Help us to know your presence with us and with them,
and strengthen our hearts by your Spirit,
that they and we may know the consolation of our fellowship
    in you,
and may hope, in due time, for the joy of reunion,
through Jesus Christ our Lord.

Family life – relationships of love

As we hear of the love of God for the Church, so we give thanks for the gift of love in our own lives. We pray for a deepening and enriching of all the relationships of love in which we share. We pray in particular for those who find tension and struggles in their family and personal relationships, and for all preparing to make public vows of love to one another.

Heavenly Father,
we give you thanks that you look on your creation with the eyes
    of love
and that you have fashioned human beings so that we can
    respond with that same love
to one another and to you.
In your mercy, deepen our delight in all our relationships of love,
help us to know your holy presence in all the moments of
    connection in our lives,
and make us more generous in sharing our love,
that those who feel alone and unwanted
may find in our care a glimpse of your endless love for them,
in Jesus Christ our Lord.

Children

Children – may we learn from them as they learn from us

Lord, we thank you for the many gifts children bring to us: for their fascination with the world; their love of learning new things; and their talent for joy and for trust. As they offer us so much, grant that we may offer them a safe environment to grow; nurture and encouragement in their explorations; and the love that will give them the confidence to flourish as their truest selves.

Lord God,
whose Son came among us as a little child
and, as an adult, saw in children the model of true faith,
bless with your love all the little ones of this earth,
that they may thrive as they grow
and find delight in the business of life,
and teach those of us who are full-grown
to care for them with the depth of your love,
for the sake of one who taught us to call you Father,
even Jesus Christ our Lord.

Youth

Youth – cooperation and respect between generations

Lord, we pray for those who are young, giving thanks for their energy and their idealism. Grant, in your mercy, that all people may be attentive and open to their insights, and may support them with wisdom and encouragement.

Lord God,
you call us all, young and old, to wait for the coming of
   your kingdom.
Help us to share with one another the gifts we have been given,
so that the old may know the energy and the trust of the young
and the young may know the wisdom and the gentleness of the old,
that together we may be found eager for the coming of
   your kingdom
and effective in pursuing justice and peace in our world,
through Jesus Christ our Lord.

Marriage

Wedding or engagement – a prayer for a couple

On this day of their wedding/engagement, we pray for N and N.
We give thanks for the gift of love that has drawn them together,
and pray that it may continue and flourish throughout their lives.

God in Trinity,
your very being is love
and you have given us the ability to find our joy and refreshment
in our relationships with others.
Be with N and N, and all those who have committed their lives to
   another, we pray,
that through their mutual support and their shared experiences
they may come to know you more deeply
as the love that binds them together,
in Jesus Christ our Lord.

Wedding or engagement – a prayer for a couple
(their love at the service of the world)

Lord, bless N and N, whom you have called together in love,
that their love may provide a source of strength for them, a sign
of encouragement to others and a motivation for their service in
the world.

God of love,
we thank you for the gift of human love in our lives,
for the ability to make relationships
and for the joy and fulfilment they provide.
Bless N and N this day with your love,
that in the joys and the struggles of life together
they would know you as the one who binds them in their unity,
and they would find in one another the fire of love,
which will kindle flames of goodness throughout our world,
through Jesus Christ our Lord.

Wedding anniversary

On this day when N and N celebrate their wedding anniversary,
we give thanks for their example of mutual commitment and for
the constant support they have provided to one another over the
years, and we pray for continued strength and well-being for them
both, and for the flourishing of all those nurturing relationships
that are at the heart of all our lives.

Lord God,
whose Son showed his love by remaining with us, whatever
    the cost,
we give thanks for the close friendship and faithfulness
that we see in the [long] marriage of N and N.
Grant to them, we pray, continued happiness in their life together,
that moved by their example
we may come to cherish ever more profoundly
all those with whom we share our lives,
in Jesus Christ our Lord.

Motherhood & Pregnancy

Motherhood – mothers (Advent: O Virgo virginum)

Lord God, as we give thanks for the central role of the Blessed
Virgin Mary in our salvation [on this eve of Christmas], so
we pray for all who are mothers. We pray for those who are
pregnant, for those who have recently given birth for the first
time, for those rejoicing in their motherhood and for those
who have difficult relationships with their children, partners
or friends, that inspired by the example of Our Lady and aided
by her prayers, they may find strength, confidence and faith in
their futures.

Almighty God,
when the time came for Mary to give birth to your Son,
a stable was the only place to shelter.
Be with all those, we pray, who are mothers,
that in times of joy and in times of sorrow,
in times of hope and in times of anxiety,
they may know the warmth of your presence with them
and the comfort of your love,
through the one born of Mary,
Jesus Christ our Lord.

Motherhood – pregnancy (The Visitation of Our Lady to Elizabeth)

[As we recall the visit of Mary to Elizabeth,] we pray for all those who are pregnant and for all who care for them and support their health and flourishing. We pray for all those who are suffering complications in pregnancy or who would love to have children but are unable to conceive, and we pray too for all new mothers, that they would be given confidence, fulfilment and joy in their care for their children.

God of life and hope,
whose Son took flesh in the womb of Mary,
grant your blessings to all those who are pregnant at this time.
Keep them in health of body and mind,
dispel from them all anxiety and fear
and help them to know your gentle power and protection,
through Jesus Christ our Lord.

Motherhood – pregnancy – difficulties in pregnancy

Lord, we pray for all those who are pregnant and for all who care for them, and especially we pray for all whose pregnancies are encountering complications, and for all couples who are struggling to conceive a child.

Lord God,
you fashion life from its very beginnings
and are with us even before we are born.
Watch over, we pray, all those who are with child,
grant them protection in all dangers,
calm in the face of all anxieties
and the help and support of family and medical professionals,
that they may find renewal in their hope for new life
and reassurance under the shelter of your wings,
through Jesus Christ our Lord.

The Gift of a Child & Parenthood

Children & parents – the joy of new life and the responsibility to care

Lord, we thank you for the wonderful gift of new life [that we celebrate today in the birth of N,] and for the joys and responsibilities of parenthood. Grant, we pray, to all who bring up children those gifts of kindness, patience, wisdom, understanding and love that bring happiness to a home and confidence to the next generation.

Lord God,
we give you thanks for the wonder of new human life,
for the beauty of the tiny baby,
the rapid development of the toddler
and the ever-growing maturity of the child.
Bless, we pray this day, all children and all parents,
that, held together in the bonds of love,
they would bring delight to one another in times of joy,
and that, held together in the bonds of patience,
they would bring comfort to one another in times of difficulty,
through Jesus Christ our Lord.

The Elderly

The elderly – those struggling with the effects of age

Lord, we pray for your world, praying especially this day for
those who are elderly, for all living in residential homes, for
all cared for by their loved ones and especially for those whose
increased frailty impedes their ability to enjoy life, and for any
who feel alone.

God of all peoples,
in your Son Jesus Christ
you show us the value of each human life
in times of strength and confidence
and in times of weakness and despair.
Be with all those who struggle this day with the effects of aging,
that they may find new ways of life and new satisfactions,
and be also with all those who care for them,
that through patience, gentleness and love
they would learn to see in the faces of those they serve
the face of Jesus Christ our Lord.

Human Tragedy

Human Tragedy of All Kinds

Human tragedy – a prayer for victims

Lord, we pray for those whose joy has been overtaken by tragedy.
Bless them with your encouragement, that they may know your
comfort, and guide them as they struggle to take the next steps on
their journey of life.

Lord, you have taught us
that in your Son the light shines in the darkness
and the darkness can never overcome it.
Be with all those whose life is overshadowed by tragedy
or dulled by hopelessness or resignation.
Help them to see the light,
however small or hidden away,
in all that they experience,
and help them to know the gentle but powerful support of
    your love,
through Jesus Christ our Lord.

Human tragedy – injury and death

Lord, we pray for all those who have been hurt this day in body, mind or spirit. Amid the pain of suffering, bring your hope, that all those in distress may find purpose and peace.

Father of all,
you hold the whole of your creation in a love that never fails.
In the midst of our anguish, help us to know your
    abiding presence,
in the midst of our mourning, help us to know your comforting
    embrace
and in the midst of our confusion, help us to know your will and
    your wisdom,
that through our friendship with you,
fragile bodies may be given strength
and broken hearts may be healed,
through Jesus Christ our Lord.

Human tragedy – loss of life

Lord, we pray for your world, a place of wonder and also a place of danger. We hold before you especially in prayer tonight the people of N and particularly all those who have lost their lives or their loved ones. We pray too for those who are injured and for all those seeking to bring help and support to a place so much in need.

Lord God,
whose world so often brings us joy
and yet is filled too with risk and pain,
hold in your everlasting arms
all those whose earthly lives were ended by ... and all
    human tragedies,
that in your eternal kingdom
they may know no more anguish,
but only the tranquillity of your presence,
and that they may know no more isolation,
but only the fellowship of your love,
through Jesus Christ our Lord.

Human tragedy – loss of home

Lord, we pray for all across the world who suffer. We pray for all those who have been displaced from their homes, any who have been injured and for those many people who have lost all they possess.

Loving God,
in your sight no human tear is unseen
and in your hearing no human cry is unheard.
Be this day with all those who suffer
while the world turns away in ignorance or carelessness.
Grant them the comfort of your presence,
the transforming gift of your hope
and the wisdom to know how to restore their lives,
and stir us from our apathy,
that we may serve them with our prayer, our time and our money,
through Jesus Christ our Lord.

Human tragedy – for an inquiry and for healing

Lord, we pray for your world. We pray for all those affected by ... and all human tragedies; for the families and friends who continue to grieve lost loved ones; for all those who bear physical and mental scars; and for all those neighbours and emergency services personnel who bear traumatic memories. We pray too for all those who lost their lives, that they would find refreshment and peace in God's heavenly kingdom.

God of all,
in whose hand each human life is held
and to whom every one of us is precious,
pour out your healing, on all those whose lives have been torn
    apart by ...
Help them to rebuild their lives and find peace,
and grant your wisdom to all who make an inquiry into the
    causes of this disaster,
that, through their work,
griefs may be aired, stories may be told,
souls may be given rest and society may be transformed,
for the sake of Jesus Christ our Lord.

Natural Disasters

Natural disasters – victims

We pray for all those whose lives this day are afflicted by the natural disasters in our news, and for all those who suffer without reaching the headlines and do not receive the help and support they need to recover.

Heavenly Father,
the whole earth is yours,
and the power of wind, wave and flame
is as nothing compared to the power of your word.
Be with all those this day who grieve the loss of loved ones
    and homes,
restore the confidence of all who are fearful for their futures
and help us all to work together to rebuild lives and restore hope,
through Jesus Christ our Lord.

Natural disasters – those whose lives have been torn apart

Lord of all, look with your mercy on all whose lives have been devastated by natural disaster, that with the strengthening power of your Spirit, and with the help of others, they may work towards a new future for themselves and their communities.

Lord God,
no human suffering is hidden from your sight
and no cry of pain goes unheard by your ears.
Be with those whose lives have been torn apart by natural disaster,
that finding consolation in their grief, and new purpose in
    their actions,
they may, with the help of charities and the support of their friends,
rebuild their lives and find wholeness and peace once again,
through Jesus Christ our Lord.

Natural disasters – flooding

Lord, we pray for your world. We pray for all people affected by flooding today, and for all those who worry about the dangers of flooding in their own communities at this time of year.

Lord of all creation,
we know that this world is a place of danger as well as of beauty,
a place of threat as well as of promise.
Defend, we pray, all those who experience or fear flooding in this
    country and beyond.
Where damage has been done, help them to rebuild,
where hopes have been destroyed, help a new future to come
    into focus,
where injuries of mind or body have been caused, help them
    to heal,
that through trust in your faithfulness
and through the gift of mutual encouragement,
communities that suffer may find new purpose, energy
    and direction,
through Jesus Christ our Lord.

Terrorism

Terrorism – the aftermath of a fatal attack

We continue to pray today for all those who have been affected
by the recent terrorist attack, for all those who have died, for all
those many people still receiving hospital treatment at this time,
and for all their families and friends. We pray for all those police
working to establish the motive for this violent act, and for those
who offer comfort and counsel to individuals in distress. We also
hold in our prayers those in our world for whom violence and
indiscriminate killing are a daily reality, for those living in war
zones, in places where the rule of law has broken down and in all
places ruled by corrupt and oppressive regimes.

Almighty God,
your love is stronger than death
and the life you offer us is everlasting.
Be a healer, we pray, to all those whom others have hurt,
be a source of peace to all those who have been traumatized,
be present in your gentleness and in your strength to those
    who mourn,
and draw, we pray, all those who have died at others' hands
into the eternal rest of your kingdom,
through Jesus Christ our Lord.

Terrorism – all victims of terrorism

Lord of all life, we pray for all victims of terrorist attacks, for
their families and friends and for all those in the emergency
services who care for them. We pray for an end to the use of
terror for political and religious purposes, for a commitment
among all people to the dignity of every single human life, and for
renewed efforts to find a future for our world that is one of peace
and harmony.

Lord, you created us for peace
and yet people have chosen war;
you made us for love
and yet so many have chosen hate.
Have mercy on the whole human race we pray,
that, through your power,
violent hearts would learn compassion,
cruelty would be replaced by tenderness
and all people would come to know the inestimable worth
of every human creature you have formed and saved,
through Jesus Christ our Lord.

Acts of Violence

Violence – an act of violence and its consequences

We pray for an end to senseless acts of violence, for a recognition
among all people of the value and dignity of every human life,
and for searching reflection on the part of legislators as to the best
ways to help prevent the repetition of such sad events.

Merciful God,
our pain is known to you
and our crying is heard by you.
Be this night with all those who suffer as a result of the violence of
    others.
Strengthen those who have been weakened in body and mind,
support those who care for wounded friends,
and draw all those who have lost their lives
into the light and peace of your kingdom,
through Jesus Christ our Lord.

Violence – victims of violence

Lord, we pray for your world. As we remember those who
suffer[ed] in N, so we pray for all those affected by the violence of
others, for those who lost their lives and all who mourn them, for
those who live on with the trauma of mind and body, for those
whose homes or communities have been destroyed, and we pray
for our future, that we may learn the paths of understanding and
of peace.

God of all nations,
who has called us to be ambassadors of reconciliation in our world,
pour out your healing on those who have suffered at
    others' hands.
Bind up the wounds of the broken,
restore the hope of the lost
and bring those who have died into the joy of your eternal presence.
Transform us all that, by learning the lessons of the past
and by growing in gentleness, compassion and respect,
we may work together for a future
in which all peoples will be set free to flourish,
through Jesus Christ our Lord.

Violence – victims and their families
(Commemoration of an atrocity)

Lord we pray for your world. As we mourn with all who lament
those they have lost in N, so we pray for an end to violence in
our world. We pray for wisdom for the leaders of the nations in
bringing these crimes to an end, for a deep appreciation among
all people of the worth of the lives of others, and for all those
tempted to violence, that they may seek the help that will allow
them to address their anger in less destructive ways.

God of love,
whose only Son was murdered as a victim of human anger and
    human pride, you hear the weeping of your children,
who grieve those they have lost.
As you comfort them in their grief, which is life-long,
do not allow us to return to our apathy as stories fade from the news.
Direct our leaders in the ways of righteousness,
show them your will for a better future
and breathe your compassion into all violent hearts,
that they may learn to accept the anger, the pain and the broken
    pride that life brings,
not by turning it into brutality towards others
but that by holding it within the Cross of your dear Son,
they may know it to be transformed into love,
in the same Jesus Christ our Lord.

War

War – for all its victims (Remembrance Sunday & Armistice Day)

Heavenly Father, we pray for our world, for all those, this day,
engaged in conflict, and for all who suffer its effects. We pray
for all survivors of conflict and all those who live with the daily
reality of pain and loss, and we pray for a commitment on the
part of the leaders of the nations to a future of peace and justice,
that we may look not to our own advantage but to the common
good of all.

Almighty God,
whose Son brought stillness to the storm
and comforted the hearts of his disciples,
bring peace and tranquillity to our earth this day.
Take away the fear that leads to violence and rashness,
and teach us all the ways of justice,
that we may seek not to seize the good things of others in selfishness
but may share all that we have in generosity,
inspired by the example and vision of your Son,
Jesus Christ our Lord.

War & terrorism

Lord, we pray for all whose lives have been devastated by acts
of war and terrorism, for those who live on with the mental and
physical scars of past conflicts and for communities ravaged by
the effects of violence. May they know your healing and new hope
for the future.

O God, the comfort of those in pain and the strength of those
    who are weak,
hold in your safe keeping this day all who have suffered through
    war and terrorism:
the wounded, the sick, the homeless, the oppressed, the anxious
    and the bereaved.
Turn the hearts of those who make for violence,
that they may learn instead the paths of peace,
for the sake of Jesus Christ our Lord.

Victims of war – save them with the strength of your arm

Lord, we pray for our world and in particular for all those
suffering the ravages of war at this time. We pray for all those
places where violence is a daily occurrence or where law and
order have broken down, and for all who work to bring peace to
them. We pray too for good relationships between the nations,
that together we may work for the peace and prosperity of
all people.

Mighty God,
there is no power on earth equal to your strength
and no intelligence on earth equal to your wisdom.
Stretch out, we pray, your arm
to protect the needy of this world.
Drive from them all who would exploit them or do them violence,
strengthen them in their pursuit of truth and happiness
and teach us all a compassion that will not look aside as
    others suffer,
for the sake of one who died at the hands of violence,
Jesus Christ our Lord.

Victims of war – be with those in trouble

Lord, we pray for all who live in places of war and terror, for those civilians held captive, for those being used as human shields, for those in hiding from oppressive governments or from the cruelty of criminals, and for those who feel themselves surrounded by personal enemies.

Lord, you hear the cry of the oppressed
and you are attentive to their need.
Show your mercy to all who live in fear of being overcome
by those stronger than themselves.
Be with them in the hidden places of their spirit,
help them to know your love for them in all their troubles,
deliver them from all who would do them harm
and help them to know that your might is greater
than the strength of all the powers of this world,
and that no one can truly be lost for ever,
through the power of the Resurrection of your Son
Jesus Christ our Lord.

The Suffering & Marginalized

Abuse

Abuse – be alongside the suffering

Lord of life, whose glory was revealed in the form of a little child, we pray for all those who are vulnerable this day. We pray in particular for those who have been abused by the cruelty of others, and especially for all who have been the victims of crime, that they may be helped to overcome the trauma of the past. We pray too for all offenders, for those in prison and for all living in our communities, for penitence and rehabilitation for them, and for all those who guide, treat and supervise their behaviour.

Lord Jesus Christ,
who came from the heights of heaven down to such a world as this,
be alongside those who have suffered the violence of others' hands
and the cruelties of others' lips.
Strengthen them in their sufferings,
that they may pursue justice and find healing.
Be too with those who have hurt and those who go on hurting,
open their eyes to the damage they inflict,
renew their compassion for the lives of others
and teach them to walk in the path that is right,
through Jesus Christ our Lord.

Abuse of the weak by the strong

Lord, we pray for your world and especially for all those who suffer at others' hands. We pray for all those who suffer abuse at the hands of family members and friends, for all who are harmed in institutions or by those who are supposed to care for them, and for all whose memories of past abuse remain traumatic and troubling.

God of love,
you taught us that the least in this world are the greatest in
   your sight,
and the weakest are those most deserving of our respect.
Be with all those today who are unable to defend themselves
against others' cruelty and lack of care.
Be a protection to them in times of danger,
be a guide to them as they consider how best to react
and be their confidence, helping them to reach out to those who
   are able to assist them.
Transform our society, our institutions, our families and our homes,
that they may be places of safety and nurture,
and make us all worthy of that great trust you have placed in
   our hands,
through Jesus Christ our Lord.

Abuse – child abuse

Lord, we pray for all children who are at risk of abuse, and for
all those in our society who work to protect them. We pray for
a willingness to listen to children's stories and a commitment
to seek the truth above all things, no matter what the cost to
reputations or institutions.

Father of all,
whose Son called the little children to come to him,
be a shield to protect all those who are small and vulnerable in
   our world.
Defend them from all who would work violence and cruelty
   against them,
grant wisdom to all those in authority, that they may bring an end
   to such brutality,
and grant to all peoples the grace to delight in and not to envy
the lives, the potential and the innocence of others,
through Jesus Christ our Lord.

Abuse – that all may flourish

Lord God, we pray for your world, for freedom for all people to flourish and to offer their talents for the common good. We pray for all who live under oppressive governments or in places where just order has broken down, for those who live in anxiety because of prejudice and for all who live in fear of violence in their own family or home.

God of light,
we thank you that you call us to worship and serve you in freedom,
that our love of you may be genuine and deep.
Deliver all who suffer
from the hands of those who would use fear to control them,
and teach your love to all who abuse their power,
that they might have the courage to open themselves to the loving
    pattern of your Son,
who revealed to us in one moment on the Cross
love's greatness and love's expense,
through the same Jesus Christ our Lord.

Betrayal

Betrayal – friend of betrayers and betrayed
(Holy Wednesday)

Lord, we pray for your world. [On this day when the Church remembers particularly the betrayal of Judas, so] we pray for all those who feel betrayed by their friends, their families or their nation. We pray too for those who feel that they have betrayed others, and also, remembering the suffering of Judas, we pray that they would know the hope of repentance, reconciliation and a more integral life.

Friend of sinners,
hope of betrayer and betrayed,
be with all those whose relationships have broken down,
those whose capacity to trust has been wounded by the acts of others
and those who, in despair, feel no longer able to trust themselves.
Help them to know your fidelity in the midst of their sufferings,
and grant that those who have been hurt might learn to trust
    others again,
and that those who have done injury might learn for themselves
    and others
the compassion for all humanity that is glimpsed in the suffering face
of Jesus Christ our Lord.

Depression & Despondency

See also Those in Pain (pp. 251–3)

Depression – befriending our needs

Lord, we pray for our world and especially for all those who
suffer its discouragements. We pray for those who feel they
have failed or disappointed others, for those who struggle to
come to terms with their circumstances, their emotions or their
selves, and for those who feel trapped in abusive relationships,
or by addictions they feel they will never control. We pray
that you would bring to them in their everyday lives people of
encouragement, who would assist them to recapture their hope
for the future and their joy in the fullness of life.

God our Creator,
you fashioned each of us before our birth
and you know our inmost hearts.
Through your mysterious providence,
help us to learn to befriend our own needs,
and bring to each one of us people who can guide and sustain us
    in our journey through life,
so that, even though we may not always see how or why,
we would be drawn closer to you each day,
through Jesus Christ our Lord.

Depression – feeling lost

Lord, we pray for your world and for all those who are especially
in need of your love this day. We pray for all who find themselves
in confusion or anxiety, for all who feel alone and uncared
for, that through your presence and our work together in our
communities, new possibilities may be made known and new
hope revealed.

God of the poor,
you hear the cry of those in need
and you are close to those who feel far from others and far
    from themselves.
Bind us together in your love,
that as one human family
we may strengthen our sisters and brothers in times of difficulty,
guide them in perplexity
and love them in moments of loneliness,
for the sake of your Son,
who knew friendship and abandonment,
joy and despair,
even Jesus Christ our Lord.

Depression & low self-esteem

As we give thanks for this place, the opportunities it offers for
service and the friendship of those around us, we pray for all
those who struggle to find purpose or companionship in life. We
pray for those who are unemployed and for all whose work is
unfulfilling or exploitative, for those who live with depression
and for those who suffer overpowering feelings of failure or
disappointment, that they would come to know joy in life and
their own inestimable worth as children of God.

Heavenly Father,
whose Son taught us that not one sparrow sold in the marketplace
  is forgotten by you,
as you formed all people before we were born,
so we pray that all people would know their worth in your eyes.
Show your mercy to those who feel that there is no meaning to
  their lives,
and help them to look on themselves as you look on them,
with eyes of love, joy and delight,
in Jesus Christ our Lord.

Depression – God in the darkness

Lord, we pray for your world and for all who find themselves in
difficulty at this time. We pray for those who are doubting what
they had previously believed in, for those living in the darkness of
mourning or grief, or the shadow of mental illness, and for those
unsure of their friendships and relationships or feeling alone,
that God's companionship would enable them to find hope and
purpose in life.

Lord God,
in your Son you have given to the world a spring of water welling
  up to eternal life.
Bring your refreshment, we pray,
to all those who struggle in the dryness of doubt and despair,
those who ache for healing but cannot find it
and those who need to know your love,
so they can have the confidence to move on in their journey
  through life,
that with the blessings of your grace,
they may find joy once again and flourish in the fullness of life,
through Jesus Christ our Lord.

Depression – be the light in the darkness

Lord, we pray for your world. [In this season of joy] we pray especially for those who find themselves unable to find happiness and contentment this day. We pray for those who suffer from anxiety, depression or mental illness of any kind, for those to whom life has brought the grief of loss of loved ones or loss of opportunities, for those who struggle to find meaning or purpose in life, that through your abiding presence and through the gentle care of others, they may come to know peace and fulfilment.

God of all healing,
who called the light to shine in the darkness at creation
and in whose eternal light there is no darkness at all,
be yourself a light of hope to those who dwell in the darkness of
    suffering this day.
Be a support to the fearful,
a listener to the lonely
and a purpose to those in despair,
that among the confusions and struggles of this world
they would find the path that leads to the fullness of life, joy and
    peace,
in Jesus Christ our Lord.

Depression – purpose in dark times

Lord, we pray for your Church, that as you hear our prayers you would offer us comfort and guidance in all we do.

Lord of love,
whose glory is a human being fully alive
and whose delight it is to know the thoughts of each living heart,
strengthen us your people when hope seems failing and faith is dim,
that, trusting in your strength alone,
we may come to know purpose in the light of the world
and joy in the water of life,
through Jesus Christ our Lord.

Depression – the cost of a vocation to life at the margins

Lord, we pray for your world and we remember especially today
those who, for whatever reason, feel themselves far off from the
friendship and fellowship of others. We pray for those who are
lonely or depressed, those who are ostracized or mocked, those
who feel themselves always marginalized or ill at ease with the
community that surrounds them.

Father of all,
you teach us that truth is so often found in the outsider
and that goodness and openness are so often found
far from where the centre of life seems to us to be.
Sustain all those whose difficult vocation it is to embody truth at
    the margins of our society,
and bring into deeper human fellowship
all those who, though now alone,
you have called to a life in the rich heart of community,
that knowing you as their companion and their inspiration,
all in their different callings
may come to know fulfilment and wholeness of life,
in Jesus Christ your Son our Lord.

The Dying & Those Who Mourn

The dying & all who await the Resurrection with longing (Eastertide)

Lord, we pray for all those who live in particular need of the hope of the Resurrection, for those facing death and for those who mourn loved ones, for those living in despair or unceasing pain and for all who cherish and care for them, and for those imprisoned by poverty or oppression, by hunger, violence or domestic abuse.

O God of Israel,
who brought your chosen people out of Egypt into the freedom of
   your promised land,
bring your liberation to all those who dwell in darkness and the
   shadow of death this day.
In your mercy,
bring hope to the dying,
comfort to those who mourn,
joy to the sorrowful,
strength to the carers,
plenty to the poor,
food to the hungry
and safety to all in peril,
that all peoples may come to know that life which is true living,
in your Son Jesus Christ our Lord.

Mourners

Lord, we pray for all those who mourn, for those shocked by a sudden death today, for those who have lost a loved one to long illness and for those whose grief has been drawn out and seems to be never-ending.

God of all comfort,
we thank you for the gift of life
and for the inspiration we find
in the lives and deaths of family, friends and all fellow humans.
Bring to those in the darkness of grief this day your light and your
    warmth,
that, enabled by the promise of your eternal love,
they would treasure in their hearts the lives of those they have lost,
and, through tears and smiles,
commit them in peace to your keeping,
in Jesus Christ our Lord.

Mourners – grant them hope and strength

Lord, we pray for your world and especially today for all who
mourn. We pray for those who mourn loved ones lost to violence
and natural disasters, for all who have lost those dear to them
in the natural course of earthly life and especially for any whose
friends or family have died suddenly or before their time. We pray
for all those who mourn in our own community, asking that as
you care for them, so you would give us the compassion and the
concern to reach out to them both in the time of their loss and in
the years ahead.

Lord of all life,
whose Son taught, 'Blessed are those who mourn, for they will
    be comforted',
look with compassion and gentleness on all who mourn this day.
Inspire them with your hope when the future seems empty
and strengthen them with your love,
that they may believe in that life which their friends now enjoy,
and come to know the fullness and richness of life for themselves
    once again,
through Jesus Christ our Lord.

Mourners – keep them from despair (All Souls' Day)

Lord of all, we pray for those who mourn, for all who have lost
loved ones [over the past year] and especially for those whose
family and friends have died at the hands of others in war, as the
victims of terrorism or of crime, that they may find healing and
peace.

Lord, we pray for those who mourn for parents and children,
for friends and neighbours.
Be gentle with them in their grief.
Show them the depths of your love
and a glimpse of the kingdom of heaven.
Keep far from them the torment of guilt and despair
and be with them as they weep,
through Jesus Christ our Lord.

The Homeless

Homeless – help us to see them as brothers and sisters

Lord God, we pray for your world. We pray especially for all
those living on the streets of this city and throughout the world,
for their safety and well-being, for their hope for the future,
and for all those organizations and institutions that try to bring
them aid.

Father of all,
you call us to be generous to those at the margins of our society
and to recognize in their faces the true image of your Son.
Give us grace that, as individuals and as communities,
we may minister friendship, healing and fresh opportunities
to those who sleep this night in the darkness and danger of
    our streets.
Give us the courage to recognize that they are our brothers
    and sisters,
the generosity to reach out to them in practical ways
and the integrity to speak up for them to those in authority,
through Jesus Christ our Lord.

Homeless – cold weather

Lord God, we pray for your world. In this time of adverse
weather we pray in particular for all who do not have the shelter
we take for granted, for those who are homeless on our streets,
for those who have no shelter across our world and for all who
seek to bring them practical support, emotional strength and
personal respect.

Lord Jesus,
whose birth was in the cold of winter
and whose death was in the cold of human indifference and scorn,
be with those who suffer the cold of this night.
Bring them to places of warmth of body and soul
through the work and the compassion of others,
that there they may experience
the restoration of flesh and spirit,
the healing of disease and pain
and the freedom to love and be loved,
for your name's sake,
O Jesus Christ our Lord.

Homeless – cold season begins

Lord, we pray for your world. As the nights begin to get colder
and the darkness longer, we remember especially those who do
not have the shelter and the light that we take for granted. We
pray for all those living on our streets in this city and country,
and for the multitudes throughout the world for whom what we
regard as basic necessities would count as luxury.

God of compassion,
in whose sight all people are equally your children,
bring your comfort to those in need this night.
Be their warmth in the cold,
their light in the darkness,
their shelter in the danger
and their companion in the loneliness,
and open all our hearts,
that in place of seeking greater abundance and security for ourselves
we would use this world's resources
to provide food, warmth and hope for all,
through Jesus Christ our Lord.

Homeless & all those vulnerable to cold weather

Lord, we pray for our world. In this bad weather, we pray for
those who have no shelter this night, those who cannot afford
heating and those for whom the cold is particularly dangerous,
and we pray too for all those in statutory bodies, charities and
Churches who seek to help and support them.

God of all,
through whom all things come into being and warmth and life,
be with all those, we pray, whose lives are threatened by cold.
Be with the homeless on our streets,
be with the elderly in cold houses,
be with the sick who need comfort and strengthening,
that by your protection, and by the efforts of us all,
they may be brought to safety, flourishing and fullness of life,
through Jesus Christ our Lord.

Homeless & marginalized

Lord, we pray for your world. We pray for those whose sufferings go unnoticed by others, for those on our streets, who we find it so easy to ignore, for those living with the pain of loneliness, who we pass by in silence, and for those multitudes throughout our world who struggle to have even what we take for granted as daily necessities. May their needs be met through our action and service.

God of us all,
whose Son taught us that we are to be neighbours to all those
    in need,
take from us the apathy that keeps us comfortable while
    others struggle
and the selfishness that leads us to obsess only over our
    own desires.
Open our eyes to all in this world that is calling for our service,
and all that we have within ourselves to offer,
that through our work and our good will
our society would be made a more generous home for all
    its members,
through Jesus Christ our Lord.

Homeless & vulnerable

Lord, we pray for your world. As we worship in the comfort and beauty of this building, we pray for all those who have nothing to protect them against the weather or the violence of others. We pray for those who are homeless here and throughout the world, for those whose accommodation is poor or dangerous and for those whose well-being is compromised by the exploitation of others. Grant to them, O Lord, your safety and your peace.

Almighty God,
you created us to live in harmony
and yet we choose to follow the path of rivalry and power.
You give us enough in this earth that all may live with dignity,
and yet we choose to hoard up things for ourselves.
Break down, we pray, all those barriers that keep us apart
    from others,
and take away our anxieties and fears,
that we may live with the openness and generosity you have
    revealed to us in creation
and taught us in the life of your Son,
Jesus Christ our Lord.

Immigrants & Refugees

Immigrants & refugees – generosity to immigrants of all kinds

Lord, we pray for your world. In times of hostility to immigrants, we pray for a more generous understanding of the needs of others throughout our world, for an openness to the value that people different from ourselves can bring to our life, and for a recognition that it is only by working together that we can serve the good and the prosperity of all.

Generous God,
to you all people are equal
and from your love nobody can be shut out.
Inspire all peoples with this vision of your equal love,
that we may learn to expand our hearts in reaching out to others
and find, by looking on their faces with gentleness,
the true image of your Son,
Jesus Christ our Lord.

Immigrants & refugees – no permanent home on earth

Lord, we pray for your world. We pray for all those who live far
from their homeland, all who have fled the violence of conflict or
civil war, those who have fled abusive relationships or neglect,
those who have to live far from their loved ones to earn a decent
wage or to have a chance of a good education, and for all
who, for whatever reason, struggle to feel comfortable in their
surroundings.

Father of all,
you have taught us that we have no permanent home on this earth
but that our true home is with you in heaven.
Comfort those who live apart from familiar places, friends
    and languages
with the knowledge of your accompanying presence,
that by drawing strength from our abiding in you,
all people may have the courage to make a home wherever they
    find themselves,
and to build an environment in which everyone can feel loved,
    supported and at rest,
through Jesus Christ our Lord.

Refugees – God close to his people on their dangerous journey

Heavenly Father, we pray for your world. We pray for all those who have been driven from their homes through war or natural disaster, through family breakdown or through the crimes of others. May they find safety, fair treatment, shelter and comfort, and be surrounded by those who can offer them care and guidance as they seek to find new beginnings and to reawaken hope.

God of all,
when your people were driven from their homes
you showed them that they could not be driven away from you
and you taught them that you would be with them wherever they
    should be.
Be with all those who make dangerous journeys of flight this day,
bring them to safety, sustain them with courage
and open the hearts of those they meet,
that they would be greeted with generosity
and guided into a new life and the hope of fresh possibilities,
through Jesus Christ our Lord.

Refugees – those who flee conflict and those determined to remain

Lord, we pray for our world and in particular for all those places where there is violence, civil strife and oppression. We pray for all those who flee their homes, that they would be granted a safe journey and a warm welcome, and we pray too for those determined to remain, that by God's protection they would find safety and comfort.

Loving God,
in your strength you watch over the weak
and in your generosity you care for those the world neglects.
Be with all who struggle this day
because of the violence and cruelty of others.
Protect those who make dangerous voyages to find a better life,
deliver those who are determined to remain in the place that is
    their home
and change the hearts of all peoples,
that together we would pursue peace
and long to live together in love and unity,
through Jesus Christ our Lord.

Refugees – exploitation

Lord, we pray for your world and especially today for an end to
the exploitation of refugees and all others who are weak. We pray
for an end to the traffic in human beings. We pray for all those
vulnerable people who find themselves in danger in their efforts to
find a better life abroad, and for the police and law-enforcement
agencies, that they may find those responsible for these terrible
crimes and hold them to account.

O God,
who cares even for the lilies of the field and the birds of the air,
and whose word teaches us that each human life is of infinite
    value to you,
be with all whose lives are reckoned cheap by those who
    exploit them.
Inspire into the hearts of the cruel and the careless
such a knowledge of your love and your judgement,
that turning aside from all that would do others harm
they would labour instead for their prosperity,
and bring into our world such peace and fairness
that all would be enabled to find what they need
to live fulfilled and joyful lives in their own place, in safety and
    in hope,
through Jesus Christ our Lord.

The Lonely

Loneliness – those who struggle

Lord, we pray for your world. We remember before you this
day all those who are lonely, those who have lost loved ones,
those housebound by pain or frailty and those who struggle to
find friends or build relationships in the midst of busy lives, that
through knowledge of your love, and through our care for them,
they would find encouragement and purpose.

God of love,
you have called us together as one people
to serve you in shared worship, joint works and relationships
    of love.
Be with all those who struggle with being alone this day,
that in the solitude they would know your constant friendship,
and that through the care of others they would know their own
    true value
and the part they can continue to play in the shared life of our
    human community,
through Jesus Christ our Lord.

Loneliness – the newly alone

We pray today for all those who find themselves on their
own after the death of a loved one, after the breakdown of a
relationship or because they have become housebound or unwell.
Help them, Lord, we pray, to find new ways of life that bring
them sustenance, enjoyment and a sense of purpose.

Heavenly Father,
your Son Jesus Christ, at times, sought out the solitude of prayer
and knew the loneliness inflicted on him by abandonment by
    his friends.
Strengthen this day, we pray, all those who find themselves alone.
Teach those who have met with loss new ways of life,
open up new possibilities for those who feel without hope
and help us all to know that you are always with us,
as our guardian, our guide and our friend,
through Jesus Christ our Lord.

Those in Need

Those in need – our privilege and their need

Lord, as we worship you in the comfort, beauty and security
of this place, so we pray for all those who do not share in these
benefits. We pray for those who are homeless, for all who are in
constant pain because of inadequate medical care, for all those
who have little to cherish or take delight in. We pray that you
would be with them in all those places of lack in their lives, that
you would show them now the abundance of your love and that
you would open our hearts, that we might be more willing to
share the good things we have with those in greater need.

Lord, you have called all humanity to the fullness of life.
Look with mercy, we pray, on all those who struggle to find joy in
    their existence.
Be a shelter to those who live on the streets,
be a comfort to those in pain,
be a friend to the lonely
and be a thing of beauty and delight to all whose life is bleak,
that your name may be glorified
and that all the peoples of this world may reflect to you
that joy and love you have in us,
through Jesus Christ our Lord.

Those in need of any kind – show them your gentleness

Lord, show your kindness to all who are in need, that as they are
met by your presence, they would find fulfilment in your love.

God of mercy,
you hear the cries of our hearts
and speak to us your words of hope with gentleness and
    encouragement.
Warm the hearts of those who struggle this day with pain
    and need.
You who are with us always,
be their protection in vulnerability,
be their comfort in distress
and be their companion in abandonment,
through the love of one who knew joy and pain,
friendship and desertion,
even Jesus Christ our Lord.

Those in need – help us to serve them

Lord, we pray for your world, for all those burdened by pain of
body and mind, for all those lacking housing or shelter and for all
who lack the income and purpose that work brings.

God our provider,
you have fashioned our world
to be an environment in which your children can flourish
    and grow.
In your gentleness,
teach us how to reach out to one another in loving service,
that, with your Spirit, we may bring
healing to the sick,
comfort to the despairing,
shelter to the homeless
and work to the unemployed,
for the sake of your Son,
who came that all may have the fullness of life,
even Jesus Christ our Lord.

Those in need – Christ's company

Lord, we pray for your world and for any who this day feel in
need of another's help. We pray for the sick and suffering, for
those lonely and afraid and for those living in poverty and hunger,
that you would accompany them and bring to them holy men and
women who would help, comfort and encourage them.

O God of all,
you love those who have least in this world,
and when they cry out in the silence you hear their prayer.
Be with all those this day who are in special need of your company,
and bring to them people
who can offer them a fresher hope and a greater sense of possibility,
that knowing your healing in the friendship and care of others,
they would be enabled to be fully alive
and share that abundant life with all those they meet,
in Jesus Christ our Lord.

Those in need – Advent and Christmas
(Advent: O Oriens)

Lord our God, [on this darkest day of the year] we pray for all
those who live without the comforts that we enjoy. We pray for
all those in this city who are homeless, all who are short of food,
those who are too poor to heat their houses and those who live
their lives in the darkness of loneliness and abandonment.

Lord God,
your Son is the light that enlightens the whole world,
and his care for those who were forced into the shadows
shows us the true meaning of what it means to live a life
radiant with the glory of God.
[As we prepare to celebrate Christmas,]
help us to shine as lights to those in need,
that through our generosity
many would be brought to share in the light of a life fully lived,
reflecting the joyful presence of God,
through the same Jesus Christ our Lord.

The Poor

The poor – those in need

Lord, we pray for your world. We remember before you all those
who live in poverty this day, all who do not have enough to eat
or drink and all who do not have the safety of shelter, that you
would protect them in their need and enable us to work together
for their welfare and for a more equal world.

God of justice,
you know the plight of the poor
and you hold them in your eternal love.
Sustain with your mercy all those who live in need this day,
and inspire our leaders and each one of us with your passion
    for justice,
that through a renewed vision of the value of each human life
and a renewed commitment to service,
we who have so much would be willing to share with those who
    have so little,
so that our world would reflect more and more
that kingdom of justice and peace,
made known to us in the teaching and life of your Son,
Jesus Christ our Lord.

The poor – Jesus himself knew poverty

Lord God, whose Son was born in the stable at Bethlehem, we
pray for all those who live in poverty this day. We pray for
the homeless, the unemployed, those who have lost everything
because of crime or disaster and for all who feel the pain of the
human poverty of loneliness. Be alongside them, that in Jesus
Christ they would come to find understanding, companionship
and hope.

Lord Jesus Christ,
in your first coming you showed us the holiness of all people
    and places
by being made flesh in the obscurity of a stable,
so be with all those who feel on the edges of society this day.
Help them to know their inestimable worth in your eyes,
help them to find the support to make the most of their gifts
    and talents,
and help us to know how best to serve them,
knowing that by serving them, we are serving you,
O Jesus Christ our Lord.

Those in Pain

Pain – be with us in its darkness

Lord, we pray for your world. We pray for those who struggle
with the darkness of pain of body and mind, for those who suffer
with chronic pain and for those who suffer with depression and
with anxiety. We pray for all who seek to support, heal and care
for them, for all family members who share the pain of those they
love and for all researching new treatments and therapies.

Loving God,
you have searched us out and known us
and you are with us wherever we may go.
Be with all those this day for whom suffering clouds the light
    of life,
warm their sadness with your company,
inflame their hope with your promise
and help them to shine as witnesses to your faithful love,
through Jesus Christ our Lord.

Pain of all kinds

Lord, we pray for all those struggling in places of darkness in our world, for all who live in loneliness or isolation, for all who suffer from depression or anxiety and for all who find their lives diminished by forces beyond their control.

God of love,
whose light brings wisdom, peace and hope,
cast away from all those who struggle
the shadows of pain and suffering.
Bring healing to the wounded,
bring insight to the confused
and bring peace to the distressed,
for the sake of your Son,
Jesus Christ our Lord.

Pain – sharing Christ's cup of suffering

Lord, we pray for your world. We pray especially today for those who share in the torment of the Cross in their own lives, for those who live in pain of body or mind, for those who live in fear of others, for those lost in this world without work, food or purpose, and for all who feel forsaken by God and unloved by others.

Merciful God,
who longs for all people to know joy and peace,
show your compassion to all who this day share in your Son's cup
    of suffering.
Deliver the oppressed from their persecutors,
heal those in pain,
restore those in poverty
and guide those in confusion,
that, seeing your light in the darkness of their world,
they may come to know the possibilities for a better future
and your constant companionship on the journey,
through Jesus Christ our Lord.

Pain – deliver us from cruelty and comfort us in difficulty

Lord, we pray for all who weep this day, for those who grieve the loss of loved ones and for all who mourn, for those who lament the breakdown of relationships and friendships and for those who cry in the pain of physical weakness or mental distress.

Loving God,
help those who suffer in this world to know your presence.
Drive away all the cruelty and violence that brings pain
and bring to wholeness all who suffer illness of mind, body or spirit,
that trusting in your promises,
and open to the light of hope,
the whole world would find this day
your gentle comfort
and your perfect peace,
through Jesus Christ our Lord.

Pain – the Passion of Christ (Passiontide & The Sacred Heart of Jesus)

Lord God, as we recall Christ's sufferings, so we pray for all those who experience deep pain this day, those afflicted by sickness of mind and body, those hurt by the cruelty of others' hands and others' words, those whom bereavement of loved ones leaves lonely and those whose loved ones bring only pain.

Lord Jesus Christ,
whose wounded heart was opened by a soldier's spear,
that all human suffering might be held within,
bring to your heart
all the pain of our lives
and all the pain of our world,
and, according to your promises,
bear it with us on your Cross,
that in our sufferings we may know that we are not alone,
and that in all human anguish remains the hope of the glory that
    is to come,
for the sake of your eternal love,
O Jesus Christ our Lord.

The Sick & their Carers

The sick

Lord, we pray for your world. We pray for your comfort and
your healing for individuals and communities suffering with
disease throughout our world.

Almighty God,
healer of the sick and strength of the weak,
look with mercy on all who suffer at this time.
Bring healing to those who are ill,
bring peace to those who are anxious,
bring strength to those who care for them
and bring wisdom to our leaders,
that they may ensure that good healthcare is available to all the
    peoples of this earth,
through Jesus Christ our Lord.

The sick (Julian of Norwich)

Lord of all, [as we recall the fever that afflicted Julian, so] we pray
for all those who are ill this day. We pray for those afflicted by
sudden pain of body or mind, those whose illnesses are long term
and wearing, and all those professionals, family-members and
friends who care for those who are unwell.

God of healing,
when our souls thirst you give us living water,
and when we are in pain you bind up our wounds and revive us.
Touch with your gentle balm all those in need of your restoration
    this day.
Bring them wholeness of body, mind and spirit,
soothe their pain
and reinvigorate them in your service,
that through your power, and the work of those who care for them,
they may find once again fullness of life, joy and peace,
through Jesus Christ our Lord.

The sick (Mary Magdalen)

Lord God, [as Mary Magdalen discovered healing through your power,] we pray for all who are in need of healing today. We pray for those who have been recently diagnosed with serious illnesses and are afraid, for those who live with chronic pain, for those whose illnesses are not visible to those around them and for all who feel alone in their sufferings, that you, Lord, would bring them healing and wholeness.

Reveal yourself, we pray, O Lord,
to all who are suffering this day.
Bring the light of your hope and healing to all places of darkness,
bring your peace to all places of anguish and restlessness
and bring the good news of your promise of eternal life
to all those whose time in this life is drawing to its close,
that in the hearts of all people
your love and mercy would be known
and your holy name would be praised,
through Jesus Christ our Lord.

The sick – an epidemic

Lord, we pray for your world. As we hear further news of the spread of N, we pray for all those affected by this disease, for healing for them, for those who have lost loved ones to this illness and for all those working to contain the infection.

Heavenly Father,
giver of life and restorer of health,
strengthen all those who suffer with N
and all those who care for them.
Grant wisdom to doctors and researchers,
insight and compassion to political leaders,
endurance to patients
and courage to family and friends,
that working together as one world community
we may overcome this disease
and bring about a healthier and more just world for those who
    come after us,
through Jesus Christ our Lord.

Carers – their need for compassion and rest

Lord, we pray for your world, for all who care for those who
are ill as family members and friends, that both carers and those
cared for would know your strength and refreshment.

God of love,
who cares for each one of your children,
bless all those who show your care to those in need.
In your mercy, teach them the value of their work.
When frustration comes, strengthen them with your gift of
    compassion,
and in all things help them to find the care they need themselves,
that through rest and support
they may be renewed in their great act of service for those they
    love,
in Jesus Christ our Lord.

Carers – care for the carers

Lord, we thank you for all those who care for others. Give them
strength in their demanding vocation of love, that as they show
your care to others, they would know your peace.

Loving God,
bless with your compassion all those who care for family
    members and friends.
Give them strength in times of tiredness,
give them calm in times of anxiety
and give them courage in times of despair,
that through their love the sick would be comforted,
relationships deepened and hope renewed,
through Jesus Christ our Lord.

Carers for loved ones who suffer – Mary's care for Jesus in his Passion (Passiontide)

Lord, we pray for all those who must look on the suffering of those they love, all who long to be able to save their children who are terminally ill, all who care for relatives whose mental or physical health is deteriorating, and all those professionals who seek to care for both the sick and their loved ones.

Lord Jesus Christ, as you died on the Cross
your mother Mary, helpless, looked on with a sorrow like
   no other.
Be with those who lament this day the pain of those dear to them.
Open to them your sacred heart of love,
give their loving grief shelter in your holy wounds,
allow them to cry by the intimacy of your presence
and wipe away their tears with the gentleness of your embrace,
that they may know, in the midst of all trouble,
that suffering and darkness will never have the last word
in a world illumined by the unfailing light of your Resurrection,
O Jesus Christ our Lord.

Wholeness & Healing

Wholeness & healing – in all contexts

Lord, we pray for all those who do not have those good things
that we enjoy. We pray for those whose lives are threatened daily
by hunger, poverty or lack of shelter, for those who live in fear
of the violence of war or oppression and for all who struggle to
find their fullness of life while coping with illnesses of mind, body
or spirit.

Lover of souls,
you called each human being to be free
and to delight in the glories of your creation.
Bring your healing, we pray, to all those people and places
in need of that wholeness and peace which comes from you alone.
Strengthen all people who bring healing, reconciliation and peace
   to others in this world,
that through their actions, and through your power,
all people may taste in this life
those joys you have prepared for us in heaven,
through Jesus Christ our Lord.

Wholeness & healing – God heals our wounds

Heavenly Father, bring your healing to all those who struggle
and suffer in life, that in you alone all people would find their
perfect peace.

God of love,
in whom all our wounds are healed
and our suffering is soothed,
send into our spirits your healing mercy,
that all that is hurting within us may be comforted
and all that is broken within us made whole,
that we would be enabled to bring to those we meet
words of encouragement, hope and peace,
through Jesus Christ our Lord.

Areas of Human Endeavour

The Arts

Arts – an arts festival

Heavenly Father, we give you thanks for our arts festival, for the inspiration of those who first conceived of it, for the many people whose work has gone into sustaining it over the years and for all who have worked so hard to make this year's festival a success. We pray for all who are taking part in whatever way, and for all who attend their events, that this festival may enrich the life of those in this city and far beyond.

Father of all,
we thank you for the manyfold gifts of the arts to enrich our lives,
for the joy they bring in times of inspiration,
for the comfort they bring in times of pain and despair
and for the power they have to bring us beyond our own experience
and deepen our knowledge, compassion and humanity.
Pour out your blessings, we pray, on this year's festival,
that through its work we may be refreshed in our spirits
and grow into deeper fellowship with all those in our community,
through Jesus Christ our Lord.

Artists – may we share your creativity

Lord God, we pray for our world. We give thanks in particular for all those involved in the creative arts, for musicians, artists and designers, for carpenters, poets and sculptors, and for all who put their inspiration at the service of others. May they be granted confidence in the value of their work, and may we who delight in it have our eyes opened to new perspectives and our hearts opened to a deeper sense of the meaning and purpose of human life.

Creator of all,
by your grace you made human beings to share in your love
   of creating
and you give us inspiration and skill to share that love with others.
Renew, we pray, the minds of all those who dedicate their lives to
   artistic creation,
that through their labours
we and all peoples would come to know
fresh insights, deeper understandings and more profound
   compassion,
through Jesus Christ our Lord.

Artists – grant them inspiration

Heavenly Father, we thank you for all who dedicate their lives to the arts. Refresh them with your Spirit, that they may continue to stimulate our wonder and insight, and may find fulfilment in all they produce.

Lord, we thank you that you have shared your creative Spirit with
    human beings,
that we, like you, may fashion things that bring delight and joy
    and peace.
Pour out richly your spirit of inspiration, we pray,
on all musicians and composers,
on all writers and thinkers,
on all painters and sculptors
and on all whose work enriches our lives and leads us to you,
and grant to each one of us, we pray,
the skill and the confidence to know how we can take part in your
    great gift of creativity,
through Jesus Christ our Lord.

Artists – fresh inspiration each day

Lord, we pray for your world. As we thank you for the wonders
you have created, we pray that you would stir up within us your
gift of creativity. Bless all those who give expression to your
glory through art of whatever kind, that enriched with heavenly
inspiration they may continue to delight and challenge us in this
shared journey of life.

God of creation,
your world is made new every morning
with fresh beauty and knowledge and possibility.
We give thanks for all that this day has brought us,
and ask that you would continue to pour out your creative Spirit
on all those who bring to expression in our hearing and before
    our eyes
that glory which is yours in eternity,
so that, stirred by their vision,
we would be set free to respond to your call,
in lives more generous, thoughtful and wise,
through Jesus Christ our Lord.

Construction Work & Construction Workers

Construction work – God our Builder

Lord, we pray for your world. [As we witness the building
work going on all around us,] we pray for all who work in
construction, for those who labour with their hands, that they
may do so in safety and with skill, for those who manage works,
that they may operate with shrewdness and compassion, and for
those who design what others build, that they would be filled with
ingenuity and a love of beauty.

God our Builder,
in whose perfect wisdom the foundations of the universe were laid
and through whose constant love
the whole order of things holds together and flourishes with life,
bless all those whose work is to create new constructions,
that with insight of mind
and deftness of hand
they may craft structures that are suited to our needs
and beautiful to our beholding,
through Jesus Christ our Lord.

Construction work – at a time of church building work

Lord, we pray for your world. [As so much building work
takes place to conserve and improve this holy place,] we pray
for all those working in construction [here at our Church and]
throughout our world. We pray for safety in their places of work,
for fairness in their treatment and for a continued growth of their
talents and understanding, that they would find fulfilment and
interest in all they do.

God our Creator,
whose wisdom conceived the order of the universe
and whose love fashioned it at the beginning of time,
bless all those who labour to construct and preserve the buildings
of our world.
In the exertion of work keep them safe and strong,
in the challenges of planning and delivery make them wise and
resourceful
and in the experience of evaluation and reflection
give them pride in their achievements
and growth in their understanding,
through Jesus Christ our Lord.

Emergency & Security Services

Emergency services – be with them as they serve us

Lord of life, we thank you for the courage shown by our
emergency services in times of danger and for their care in times
of human weakness. We pray that you would be alongside them
as they carry out their duties, that you would help them to know
your presence with them in all they do, and that you would show
them that through their service to others they are serving you.

Lord God,
your Son taught us that what we do for the least of our brothers
and sisters
we do for him also.
Strengthen those who spend their lives in the service of others,
be their defender when they protect others from harm,
be their steadfastness when they work long hours
and be their friend when they need care themselves,
through one who came not to be served but to serve,
even Jesus Christ our Lord.

Security services of all kinds – protect them in danger

Lord, [in a time of uncertainty and danger in our world,] we pray for all those who put themselves at risk for the sake of others, for all soldiers working to defend the rights and dignity of civilians, for police working to protect society and for all those working in security, who put themselves in places of difficulty that we may live in safety. We pray that you would be with them now to comfort and reassure them, to deliver them from all who wish them harm and to help them know the high value of their work.

Almighty God,
protector of all who put their trust in you,
we commend to your goodness this day
all who put themselves in danger for the service of others.
Be their strength when they are in peril,
give them confidence to commit their lives to your protection,
and through their work let the good triumph
and all evil and cruelty flee away,
for the sake of our Saviour, Jesus Christ our Lord.

Farming

Farming – harvest

Lord, [as we give you thanks for the gifts of the harvest, so] we pray for those who do not have enough. We pray especially for all those farmers in this and every land who, while providing us with abundant and cheap food, struggle to make their own livelihoods viable. We pray for all those in our own society who need to make use of foodbanks and charitable meals to feed themselves and their families, and for those multitudes throughout our world who are not even able to enjoy the essential sustenance we take for granted here.

Lord of the harvest,
we thank you for those good gifts that you have given us.
As we draw strength and delight from our food,
so help us not to forget
the labour of those who made it,
the conditions in which they work
and the burning needs of the hungry,
that inspired by your generosity to us
we may fashion a more generous and fairer world
for our fellow human beings today and for all those who come
    after us,
through Jesus Christ our Lord.

Farming (Rogation) – preserving the fruitfulness of the earth for the future

Lord of all, we pray for your world. [On this rogation day] we
pray for the fruitfulness of the earth and for the wise management
of the land and of the world's environment, that they may
continue to bear fruit for generations to come. We pray too
for the fair treatment of all who work in agriculture and food
production, and for the generous sharing of this earth's resources,
that all may have enough.

Lord of the harvest,
without whom nothing that is wholesome can grow
and nothing that is pleasing can flower,
bless the fertility of our earth,
that it may bear fruit in abundance for your people.
Guide and direct the labours of those who work on it,
and all those leaders who are entrusted with its care,
that it may be a source of food,
a place of beauty
and a true home,
for us and for all who come after us in the years ahead,
through Jesus Christ our Lord.

Farming (Rogation) – may the earth's creatures be fruitful and multiply

Lord, we pray for your world. [On this rogation day] we give thanks for the beauty of the earth, its fruitfulness and for all the many ways it enables and nurtures life. We pray for all who work with the earth, to farm it, to conserve it, to mine it and to build on it, that they may do so in ways that are sustainable and life-giving for both humanity and the environment. And we pray for our leaders, that in their decision-making they may seek to preserve this invaluable resource for future generations.

God of glory,
who created the earth to share in the beauty of the heavens,
bless our land and all that thrives on it.
May our world teem with life,
may its creatures be fruitful and multiply,
may it yield in season a plentiful harvest
and may we work to enable it to flourish and grow
now and for the generations to come,
through Jesus Christ our Lord.

Finance

Financial services

Lord, we pray for your world. We pray in particular today for all those who work in commerce, for the life of all financial centres, for wisdom for them in all that they do, and for integrity and responsibility in their management of so much of the world's wealth.

Heavenly Father,
you have taught us to share our gifts for the good of all
and have given each one of us talents that can be used for the
    benefit of our communities.
Bless all those who work in our financial markets,
that they may be astute in their judgements,
responsible in their business practices
and compassionate in their use of wealth,
through one who called the rich to hear the cries of the poor,
even Jesus Christ our Lord.

The Media

Media – wisdom and encouragement

O God, we pray for all those who work in our media, that they
may speak the truth with diligence and with compassion.

Almighty God,
we thank you for those who devote their lives to the work
    of journalism,
for those who write articles,
for those involved with printing and online publication,
and for those whose work ensures
the efficient management and continued financial viability of
    our media.
Grant to them, O Lord, a spirit of right judgement in all things,
satisfaction in the craft of accurate reporting and engaging writing,
a love for the truth
and a delight in the community they are called to serve,
through Jesus Christ our Lord.

Media – courage and integrity of journalists in places of oppression

Lord, we pray for all who work in our media, and especially today for all those courageous journalists who work in places of oppression or state-controlled media.

Lord God,
we thank you for all who seek to bring truth to others,
and especially for the bravery of those who report from
   dangerous lands
and those who dare to speak of realities that governments wish
   to hide.
Grant them your Spirit of insight,
that they may be enabled to see clearly in times of confusion,
and your Spirit of wisdom,
that they may present what they have learnt
in ways that build up and do not destroy,
through the messenger of the covenant,
Jesus Christ our Lord.

Medicine

Medicine – all those who work in medicine (St Luke)

Heavenly Father, [as we recall Luke the Physician, so] we pray for all those who work in medicine in our day, for those who work directly in the care of others as doctors, nurses, therapists and carers, for those whose research finds out new treatments and cures for our sicknesses and infirmities, and for those whose simple offering of love and friendship brings healing of souls and hearts.

Loving God,
we thank you for your gift of healing,
brought to us so often through the work of others.
Deepen them, we pray, in their skills,
give them creativity and insight in their work,
help them to see those who suffer with your eyes of compassion,
so that through their generous care,
lives would be restored and hope would be renewed,
through Jesus Christ our Lord.

Medicine – health workers

Lord, we thank you for all those whose vocation it is to support the health of others. We pray for all doctors, nurses, therapists and professional carers, and for all those who support their work, that through their skill and their kindness, many would be brought to health and wholeness this day.

Almighty God,
whose Son came to heal the sick and tend to those in need,
bless all those who, following his example,
commit their lives to acts of kindness and mercy,
that, through their ministry,
wounds may be healed,
spirits may be lifted
and pain may be comforted by love,
through Jesus Christ our Lord.

Medicine – medical research

Lord of wisdom, we pray for all those working in medical
research, that through their labours new cures and treatments
may be found for many of the diseases that cause such pain and
misery among your children. We pray for the proper funding of
research by public and private institutions, for the fair treatment
of all who work in science, and for balance, honesty and integrity
in the reporting and use of the results they obtain.

God of all knowledge,
through whom all truth is made known,
bless with your insight all those researchers working strenuously
to find cures for this world's diseases.
Guide and strengthen them with your wisdom
and bring their labour to its fruition,
that through their work
ever more people would be enabled to enjoy that fullness of life
    which is your will for us,
in Jesus Christ our Lord.

Medicine – the National Health Service

Lord God, we give you thanks for the courage, commitment
and compassion of all who work in our emergency services,
and in particular for all those working in our National Health
Service. We pray for all health professionals, all administrators
and managers, all drivers and porters and all whose care saves
lives and restores health. We pray too for our legislators and
government, that they would have your gifts of wisdom and
sensitivity as they plan for the increased demands and challenges
to the NHS that our future will bring.

God of healing,
through your generosity
you have given us your wisdom to heal,
and through your inspiration
you have given us the ability to care.
Be with all those who work to preserve the health of others
and all who support their labours.
In their times of tiredness, be their refreshment,
in their times of confusion and panic, be their calm,
in their times of dejection and beleaguerment, be their hope,
for in you is our hope and our wholeness,
through Jesus Christ our Lord.

Medicine – the National Health Service over Christmas

God of all, [in this time of particular demand on our National
Health Service,] we pray for all those who dedicate their lives to
the care of the sick. We give thanks for those who work [over
the Christmas and New Year period] in hospitals, clinics and
ambulances, to preserve life and bring healing [, and we pray
for all medical staff who work under the increased pressure that
this season of the year brings]. Amid the busyness and hurry of
their work, give them, we pray, wisdom in their judgements,
compassion in their care and fulfilment in all that they do.

Healing God,
whose Son Jesus brought wholeness to lives
through the gentleness of touch and the power of love,
pour out, we pray, your power to heal on all those who work
    in medicine,
that through your mercy
we may see in our own day
the injured returned to health,
the distressed led to happiness
and the broken restored to wholeness,
through Jesus Christ our Lord.

Medicine – thanksgiving for the National Health Service

Lord, we give thanks for the dedication of all those who have
served the health and well-being of this nation over so many
years in the National Health Service, for doctors and nurses, for
therapists and technicians and for all who manage and support
their work. We pray too for the future of the NHS, that through
the support of government, patients and staff it may continue
to flourish and develop to meet the challenges future years
will bring.

God of healing,
you bind up our wounds and revive us,
and when we are in pain you hold us in your loving arms.
We thank you for the commitment, skill and compassion of so
    many people
who have served the NHS over the years that have passed,
and we pray that, through your gift of wisdom,
our health service would be prepared to face the future
with confidence, with purpose and with hope,
through Jesus Christ our Lord.

Rest & Travel

Rest is a good thing – the Sabbath

Creator of all, who saw that all creation was good and took rest
on the seventh day, we give thanks for the gift of this Sabbath
day, for its opportunities for worship and for fellowship with
one another, and for the power of rest to restore us and make us
whole again. We pray that we may have proper respect for the
need to take rest from our labours. We pray for the safety and
happiness of those on holiday at this time, and for all who do
not have the opportunity for rest because of poverty or unfair
working conditions.

Lord of the Sabbath,
we thank you that in times of quiet we find our re-creation for
   your service.
Help us to keep your command to respect the dignity of rest as
   much as work,
teach us where we can find opportunities for relaxation in the
   busyness of life,
give us the courage and sense of proportion to make the most
   of them
and help us to work together for a world
in which time for relaxation and the cultivation of friendships and
   family ties
would be not the privilege of the rich
but the common property of all,
through Jesus Christ our Lord.

Rest – the dignity and purpose of the holidays

Lord, we pray for all those who take holidays and travel at this
time, for their safety, their refreshment and their relationships
with those with whom they spend time.

God of the Sabbath,
in your resting from creation you show us the dignity and holiness
   of relaxation
and its power to re-create our own strength and creativity.
Grant to all those who take holiday at this time
the calm of soul to find peace,
the excitement of mind to explore new places
and the friendship of heart to grow in understanding and love
of those with whom they travel,
that their time away would bear much fruit in their own lives and
   the lives of others,
through Jesus Christ our Lord.

Travel

We pray for all those taking holidays at this time, that they may
travel in safety. We pray that their time away may be one of
rest and relaxation, and that they may grow in fellowship and
understanding with their travelling companions and with all who
are their hosts in their holidays.

Lord of all creation,
you made a world rich in diversity,
a world so large that we can never hope to see it all.
We pray that, through our travel,
we may grow in sympathy for those different from ourselves,
that we may come to know more intimately those with whom we
    share our lives
and that we may come to learn the dignity and importance of rest
and of care for the soul,
through Jesus Christ our Lord.

Science & Scholarship

Science & scholarship – researchers

Heavenly Father, as we thank you for the wonder of all creation,
so we pray that our understanding of it may grow and be guided
by your goodness. We give thanks for all those who study nature
through the sciences and for all who probe the questions of our
history, and the structures and meaning of our existence, through
the humanities. Help us, we pray, to use their work rightly, for
the service rather than the destruction of others, and grant that in
our searching for truth we may discover more of you, for you are
truth itself.

Lord God,
you have given human beings the intelligence to understand
   something of nature
and the curiosity to investigate the structure of your creation.
Guide us, we pray, in our seeking after truth,
that our knowledge may be put to good purposes
and our moral instincts may be sharpened and deepened
by our ever greater comprehension of this world
and our ever greater reverence for the wonder of humanity,
through Jesus Christ our Lord.

Sport

Sport – for all athletes

Lord, we pray for all professional athletes, giving thanks for their
dedication and their skill and for the excitement their endeavours
provide to others. We pray too for all amateur sports and for all
involved in junior and school sport, that they would lead to a
spirit of fellowship among individuals and a training in working
together, that in the public realm and in private life we may come
to recognize more profoundly our reliance on and our obligations
to one another.

Lord of all life,
we thank you for the gift of our bodies,
for their potential to develop and grow in strength and dexterity,
and for those people whose training and talent
produce performances that are delightful and inspiring to watch.
Teach us all to reverence these gifts you have given us,
that through all our life we may become fully alive in body as well
   as in mind,
and learn to be gentle and patient when our bodies need care,
through Jesus Christ our Lord.

Sport – a sporting competition

Lord, we pray for your world. [As we celebrate N, so] we give
thanks for the commitment, skill and excellence of athletes, and
pray for their safety and fulfilment. We pray for all involved with
coaching and managing sports teams, that they would do so with
integrity and care, and for all young people involved in sport at
any level, that through their activities they would grow in fitness,
friendship and talent.

Creator of all,
you fashioned humanity to rejoice in skills of mind and body
and you give us the energy and aptitude
to compete in peace and to delight in achievement.
Be with all those who take part in this competition
and with all who inspire us with their dedication and skill in sport,
that in their accomplishments
we may appreciate the wonder of your human creation
and know your generosity and your care,
through Jesus Christ our Lord.

Work & Unemployment

Work – fair treatment

Father of all, we pray that all people may flourish in their
employment. We pray for good relationships in the workplace,
for fair pay and just working conditions, and for blessings
in times of rest and holiday. We pray too for all who are
unemployed and those struggling to find enough hours of work
to make ends meet, that they would be given the personal and
professional support they need to move forward in their lives.

Heavenly Father,
whose work is the whole of creation,
we thank you for the skill and intelligence you have given us,
for the fulfilment and creativity we can find in work
and for the colleagues who encourage us in all that we do.
Bless us as we work, that we may reflect your creative love for
    the world,
bring justice to those who work in unfair or unsafe conditions,
find employment for all who are without it
and give opportunities for rest and re-creation to all,
through Jesus Christ our Lord.

Work – encouragement and purpose in our labour (St Joseph)

Lord God, we pray for your world. [As we recall Joseph's
labour as a carpenter in Nazareth, so] we pray this day for all
working people, that we would find fulfilment and purpose in
our occupation and a proper balance of work and the rest of life.
We pray for all who work in dangerous conditions, for those
whose labour is exploited and for all who find work stressful,
exhausting or isolating.

God our redeemer,
whose Son knew the dignity of Joseph's labour
and who calls us each day to put our hands to the service of
    the world,
show us, in our work, something of your purpose in our lives.
In times of dryness and futility, give us your hope,
in times of anxiety and overload, give us your peace,
in times of confusion and uncertainty, give us your guidance,
and help us to work together
for a world of greater justice, opportunity and prosperity for all,
through Jesus Christ our Lord.

Work – financial worries

Lord, we pray for all those who are worried about their finances today, for those concerned about supporting themselves or their families, for those anxious about businesses for which they have responsibility, and for those in government concerned about the wealth of our nation and of our world. Grant to them calm and clarity of judgement, that all people may know how best to seek security for themselves and for all those for whom they care.

God of plenty
and sustainer of those in distress,
comfort all those who are anxious about their financial situation.
Direct our leaders in ways of wisdom and compassion,
direct our businesses in ways of shrewdness and understanding,
direct each one of us in ways of generosity and care,
that through our concern for one another,
individuals, organizations and our whole society
would be given the strength to endure present challenges
and to work towards a shared future with hope,
through Jesus Christ our Lord.

Work – safety at work

Lord, we pray for your world. We pray for all those who work in dangerous conditions, for care and responsibility in management to help them to work safely, and for all who work in countries where lax regulations expose them daily to the risk of harm.

God of all,
who protects the lives even of the lilies of the field
and who seeks after the one sheep that is lost, even from the flock
    of one hundred,
save and defend all those whose work is dangerous.
Guide them in their labours
and direct their managers in compassion and wisdom,
that all may be enabled to earn their living
in ways that are safe, healthy and productive,
through Jesus Christ our Lord.

Work – satisfaction in labour

Creator of the universe, we pray that all people would find
satisfaction in their employment and be treated fairly by their
employers. We pray for good relations between management and
employees, especially where they have become strained, and we
pray for any who find work stressful or meaningless, for those
who work anti-social hours and for those forced by coercion
or by financial necessity to work against their will or in unsafe
conditions. We pray for all those seeking work and for all who
are struggling with unemployment at this time.

Father of all things,
who created the world by your power and said, 'it is very good',
we pray that all people may find like satisfaction in their labour,
that they would know the value and significance of their input
    to society,
that they would be justly and fairly treated in their work
and that through their effort their talents would become manifest
    and be enabled to grow,
through Jesus Christ our Lord.

Work – the value of labour

Heavenly Father, we pray for all who work. We pray especially
for any who find their work stressful, for those who work for
unfair pay and for those who work in dangerous conditions. We
pray for greater justice and compassion in all places of work, for
a recognition of the value of everybody's labour and for a greater
sense of the common good in the management of all businesses.

Father of all,
we thank you for the opportunities for productivity and
    fellowship that work provides,
and for those talents you have given us to serve one another.
Strengthen us and all who work,
whatever our calling,
that all our labour may bear fruit
in improved societies, fairer communities and deeper human
    relationships,
through Jesus Christ our Lord.

Unemployment – help them to find new work

God of all, [as we hear of job losses, so] we pray for all those
affected by unemployment. We pray for those who have
recently lost a job or who are about to do so, for the long-term
unemployed, for those who live in fear of unemployment because
of business conditions and for all those whose work is unreliable.
We pray too for those who seek to support others in finding work
in job centres and through personal connections and advice.

Lord, you made humanity with the skill to serve others in work,
and help us through our labour to discover new gifts and talents.
Strengthen all those who long for work but cannot find it,
give them the skills of presentation and commitment they need to
    find new employment
and bring them wise and discerning advisors,
that through their new occupation they would be able to make
    their living
and find new opportunities, friends and purpose in life,
through Jesus Christ our Lord.

Education

Teaching & Learning: Students

Students – the gift of learning

Lord, we pray for all students. As we thank you for all that they bring to the common life of our society, so we pray that they would be renewed by your spirit of wisdom in their studies, their projects, their extra-curricular activities and their social life.

Lord of wisdom,
we thank you for the gift of learning,
through which we discover more profoundly the truth of you, the
    world and ourselves.
Grant, we pray, to all those who study,
skill and knowledge in their work,
enthusiasm and interest in their subject
and refreshment and joy in the company of others,
through Jesus Christ our Lord.

Students – learning throughout life
(A teacher of the faith)

Lord, [on this day when we celebrate the teaching ministry of
N,] we pray for all who teach and all who learn. We pray for
all young people, that through their studies they would grow in
maturity, in wisdom and in skill. We give thanks for all teachers,
coaches and youth workers, and pray that their important
vocations in life may nurture their own creativity and sense of
fulfilment, and we pray for all those who teach others in informal
ways the meaning of a life well lived.

Lord, we thank you for the gift of learning
and for the opportunities it gives us all to discover a broader
    perspective on our world.
Teach us with your gentle wisdom,
that through all our studies and through all our interaction
    with others
we may draw closer to you in truth, in beauty and in goodness,
through Jesus Christ our Lord.

Students – freshers

Lord of all peoples, we pray for our community and especially for
all those students new to this city at this time. We pray for any
who are anxious or uncertain about what lies ahead, and for any
who are lonely, that they would find trust in your mercy and joy
in the company of others.

Lord of all wisdom,
who has given us the intellect to learn, understand and explore,
be with all those who are beginning a new stage of their education
    this week.
Grant them the confidence to form new friendships and to make a
    new home,
grant them the discernment to make the most of the time they
    have at university,
grant them your protection to keep them from all harm,
and help us to welcome them into the common life of this place,
through Jesus Christ our Lord.

Students – seeking truth and pursuing it

Lord, we thank you for the gift of learning and we pray for all
who study, all who teach and all who support their work, that a
new generation would discover an ever deeper love for truth and
an ever greater compassion for others.

Lord God,
yours are the depths of all wisdom and knowledge.
Be with us all as we seek after truth
in our studies, our relationships and our experiences.
Give us your gift of discernment, we pray, to see where truth lies,
that we may know what is right,
that we may love it with undivided hearts
and that we may pass on what we have discovered to those that
   come after us,
through one who is himself the wisdom of God,
even Jesus Christ our Lord.

Students – exam results

Lord of all wisdom, we pray for all those who are receiving their
exam results today and for their futures. We pray in particular for
any who have received bad news today and are having to change
their plans at short notice, and for any anxious about what lies
next for them in their lives. We give thanks too for the joy of all
those who have achieved and exceeded their expectations.

Lord of all truth,
we thank you that on our path through life
you enable us to grow in knowledge, skill and maturity.
Be with all those this day who are preparing to take the next step
   on their journey,
strengthen those whose next move is uncertain
or who are disappointed at possibilities suddenly closed off,
and remind us all this day that your plan for us is more profound
   and more truthful
than any pathway that we could construct for ourselves,
through Jesus Christ our Lord.

Teaching & Learning: Teachers

Teachers (St Basil & St Gregory)

Lord, we pray for your world. [As we give thanks for Basil
and Gregory, so] we pray for all who teach in our schools,
universities, churches and homes, and for all those who give us
encouragement and direction by the goodness of their actions and
the beauty of their characters.

O God, who delights to teach us wisdom by the words and
    example of others,
strengthen all those who guide the people in their care.
Grant to all teachers a love of truth,
an enthusiasm to inspire
and a heartfelt concern for those committed to their charge,
that those who learn would grow in sensitivity, in knowledge
    and in maturity,
and grant us all the grace of openness,
to discover the new insights we can learn from those around us
and the fresh possibilities that lie open to us each day,
through the power of your transforming love,
made known to us in Jesus Christ our Lord.

School Life: End of Year

See also Rest & Travel (pp. 272–4)

School – end of year – the changing seasons of life

We pray for all those for whom the end of this academic year
marks an important transition in life, for those leaving or
changing school or university, those making a start in the world
of work, those who are changing jobs and those who are retiring.
Grant to each, we pray, O Lord, the knowledge of your ongoing
presence with them. Calm their anxieties and help them to find
excitement and purpose in all that they are about to take on.

Lord, you have taught us that there is a time for all things:
a time to plant and a time to pluck up what is planted,
a time to seek and a time to lose,
a time to weep and a time to laugh.
Be with us, we pray, through all the changing seasons of our lives,
that as we go on in years
and as we experience change,
so we would grow in maturity,
deepen in compassion
and be enriched in humanity,
that we would learn day by day
what it is you have called us to be,
in Jesus Christ our Lord.

School – end of year – leavers

Lord, we pray for your world. As the summer holidays begin,
we pray that all those on vacation may find a time of rest and
recreation, and we pray especially for all those moving on to new
chapters in their lives, and for all inhabiting a time of transition
this year. We pray for all moving to new schools, new jobs and
new life-stages, that in those places they may continue to know
your presence, which calls us constantly towards new horizons
and fresh wisdom.

Lord of all time and space,
be with us in this world of change.
Comfort us in the sorrow of departure,
excite us in the thrill of adventure
and direct us in the discernment of our future,
that through your strength
and through the friendship of those around us,
we may walk with confidence the path of life,
this day, in the years to come and to our days' end,
in the company of Jesus Christ our Lord.

Social Virtues

Civility & Kindness

Civility – speak with kindness (St James the Great)

Lord God, we pray for your world. [As we recall St James'
concern for the right use of speech, so] we pray for your guidance
on all that is spoken in our world. We pray for our leaders, that
they would speak with wisdom and integrity, for those in the
media, that they would speak with freedom and truthfulness, and
for each one of us in our daily lives, that we would minister to one
another words that do not destroy and undermine but which seek
to build up and encourage.

God our Father,
who gave us the gift of speech,
that we might tell of your truth
and speak to one another of the deepest thoughts of our hearts,
bless all the speaking of this world.
Take from our mouths all words of anger and cursing
and in their place let there flow tenderness and concern;
take from our mouths all words of hatred and pride
and in their place let there flow love and humility;
take from our mouths all words of humiliation and contempt
and in their place let there flow respect and esteem,
that all our speech would be a spring of water, fresh, nourishing
    and clean,
reaching out to advise and strengthen those around us,
through Jesus Christ our Lord.

Encouragement & Gratitude

Encouragement & gratitude – those in need of encouragement

Lord, we pray for your world, remembering especially those who do not receive the recognition and thanks they deserve. We pray for those working for low pay, for those treated unfairly by their employers or overlooked or neglected by their colleagues, for those whose constant care sustains the life and health of others but leaves them feeling alone and ignored.

God of grace,
we are yours, and you know us each by name.
In our world of exploitation and alienation,
help us to learn your gift of gratitude.
Remind us to reach out to one another constantly in thanksgiving
    and encouragement,
and show to those who feel alone, unloved or overlooked
your delight in their existence,
your interest in their thoughts and feelings
and your purpose for their lives,
in Jesus Christ our Lord.

Encouragement & gratitude – gratitude for the under-acknowledged

Lord, we pray for all those who offer support and encouragement to others while not seeking attention and acclaim for themselves. We pray for all family members whose partners, children or parents need their support because of their public role, and we pray for all whose job involves supporting others as personal assistants, administrators and managers, that they would find fulfilment in their work and recognition for their important roles.

God of all,
in the Gospels you show us the dignity
of welcoming, caring for and assisting others in their vocations,
and the importance of the networks of friendship and relationship
that enable each person to flourish.
In an age of celebrity and the cult of self-publicity,
give your support to those whose role in life or in work is the
    quiet support of others,
that, through their ministry, the common good would be
    furthered,
and their own lives and the lives of those they care for
would be set free to serve this world
with confidence and with joy,
through Jesus Christ our Lord.

Equality & an End to Prejudice

Equality – caring equally for all

Lord, we pray for justice and peace throughout the world, for
a fairer sharing of the world's resources, for a commitment
to care for the environment and to care equally for our fellow
human beings.

God of us all,
we thank you for this world's rich diversity,
for its many cultures, peoples and languages,
for its wonderful range of creativity
and for the human capacity to share, to nurture and to love.
Help us to live, as you would wish, as one family,
unafraid of difference
and open to seeing, in the faces of those most unlike ourselves,
the face of your precious Son,
Jesus Christ our Lord.

Equality – an end to discrimination

Lord, we pray for an end to persecution and prejudice on the
grounds of faith, politics, race, gender or sexuality. We pray for
all prisoners of conscience, for all whose safety is neglected or
deliberately ignored by those in authority, and for the work of
Amnesty International and all charities dedicated to restoring
human dignity across our world.

God of all,
of Jew and Greek,
of slave and free,
of male and female,
bring our human eyes to see the world as you see it.
Liberate us from the fear that makes us discriminate against others,
and bring to safety all those who suffer the violent consequences
    of prejudice,
that we may know, in our day,
our world remade as one
and all humanity united in love,
through the power of Jesus Christ our Lord.

Equality – all are brothers and sisters

Lord, we pray for your world. We pray for all repressed
minorities this day, for all who suffer state-sponsored oppression,
casual violence, ridicule or reduced rights, and for all who work
for a world in which every human being is treated with an equal
respect.

God of creativity,
by your inspiration you give us the power to rouse souls and
    change nations.
Stir up in us that deep compassion for one another
that makes us see all your children as our brothers and sisters.
Teach us to fight the temptations of prejudice and pride
with the strength of truth and openness,
and bring about in our world that kingdom of peace and justice
which is the longing of the hearts of the poor,
through Jesus Christ our Lord.

Equality – the temptations of prejudice

Lord, we pray for our world. We pray for greater mutual respect between people of all religions, cultures and backgrounds in this and every land. We pray for a genuine recognition that no group of human beings is fair game for insults, abuse and insinuation, and for a spirit of greater determination to put an end to the acceptability of prejudice in some parts of our society.

God of us all,
we pray for your family on earth,
so often at war with itself,
so often preferring the easy answers of prejudice
to the deep understanding required by love.
Give us all grace to open our eyes to the insights of others,
and open our hearts to the raw humanity of their experiences,
that together we may build a society that works in the interests
    of all,
through Jesus Christ our Lord.

Equality – overcoming hatred and division (St Stephen)

Lord God, we pray for all places where people are persecuted for
their religious or political beliefs, or for their cultural or racial
background. [As we remember the cruel death of St Stephen,
who stood firm in his faith,] we pray for renewed respect for
one another in our own day, for the grace to learn from those
different from ourselves and for the humility to serve them with
love and attentiveness.

Heavenly Father,
the birth of your Son as a little child calls each one of us
to recall our own fragility and our dependence on you.
Help all peoples to be open to your care
and aware of the riches that lie in opening our own hearts to others.
Give us compassion that we may invite all peoples into the
    warmth of our company,
give us wisdom that we may see what is good in all traditions
    and beliefs
and give us love, that we might overcome all those barriers that
    keep us apart
and be one people, one family,
redeemed through Jesus Christ our Lord.

Equality – forced marriage (St Agnes and other martyrs)

Lord, we pray for your world. [As we recall that Agnes was killed
because of her refusal to enter a forced marriage, so] we pray
for all those forced into unwanted relationships this day. We
pray for an end to coerced marriages and the so called honour-
based violence that enforces them, for a renewed respect for the
rights of all, especially women and girls, to autonomy over their
own bodies, and for a renewed effort on the part of national
governments and the United Nations to bring greater freedom to
individuals in their personal lives.

God of love,
you show us that love itself is a gift which can never be compelled,
and in your gentleness you offer us complete freedom in our
    relationship with you.
Teach the world, we pray, this truth about love.
Bring an end to the violent trading of others' lives
and to the unwillingness to hear the protesting voices and stories
    of suffering of the young,
and show us how, by protecting one another,
we can nurture relationships and build a society
in which justice and righteousness are at home,
through Jesus Christ our Lord.

Hope

Hope

Lord of all, we pray for the gift of hope in our world of doubt and
despair. We give thanks for all that is good in human life and pray
that you would renew our perspective, so that all people would
choose to live in hope rather than fear. We pray for all those
places where hope seems particularly difficult to cling on to, for
places long ravaged by war and violence, for places of devastating
poverty and hunger, and for homes in which disorder and cruelty
seem to reign. Through your healing, renew our hearts and help
us all to work together for a better future.

Lord of all,
you call your children to live in hope,
in the knowledge that you alone are our beginning and our end,
our goal and our purpose in life.
Refresh all hearts that are weary this night with your gifts of rest
    and restoration,
that we may awake to a new day,
alive to its possibilities,
excited by its opportunities
and committed in it to the service of others,
in Jesus Christ our Lord.

Hope – the light that darkness will never overcome
(St John, Apostle and Evangelist)

Lord God, [even as St John speaks of the compassion and healing
brought by Jesus, he reminds us that we are not all open to the
freedom he came to bring. And so] we pray for your world, for
all places where darkness seems to have the upper hand, for all
places where government is corrupt, where the police are violent,
where those who are rich abuse their power and go unpunished,
that those places may know your peace and justice once again.

Lord Jesus Christ,
you are the light that shines in the darkness,
the light that the darkness cannot overcome or even comprehend.
Shine brightly, we pray, in all places of sadness this day.
With your bright beams drive out the shadows of cruelty
    and violence,
clear away the gloom of confusion and hopelessness
and shatter the night of fear,
that however small hope for a better future may seem,
all people may find comfort and purpose in that flame of love
which you nurture in our hearts,
for you are this world's light, love and life,
O Jesus Christ our Lord.

Hope – urgent hope for the coming of Christ
(Advent: O Emmanuel)

Lord God, we pray for our world, for all those who look for
salvation in the daily trials of their lives and for those who need
especially to hear your words of hope and deliverance. We pray
for those struggling in their relationships, those who are lonely
or depressed and those who live in the shadow of violence or the
pain of mourning.

Lord Jesus Christ,
come among us and deliver us from all that binds us,
scatter the darkness of sorrow with the light of your presence,
dispel the fear of others with the knowledge of your love
and deliver all who suffer from the hands of those who do
    them harm,
that throughout the whole world
all people may come to enjoy that kingdom of peace and justice
of which your coming is a sign,
that throughout all nations your joy would be known and your
    name would be praised,
O Jesus Christ our Lord.

Open-mindedness & Tolerance

Open-mindedness – help us to see the complexity of life (St Thomas)

Lord Jesus Christ, [whose apostle St Thomas had the courage to doubt for a time what he was told by his friends,] in a world of increasingly inflexible certainties of belief and politics, where to question or to be uncertain is often criticized as treachery, help us all to recover our respect for doubting, for seeing both sides of an argument and for people who think differently from ourselves.

Heavenly Father,
[as Thomas found a deeper assurance in his faith through
    his doubts,]
grant to all people, in our public and private lives,
a breadth of vision that enables us to see the rich complexities
    and nuances
of the many challenges that face our society.
Keep us from the temptations of simplistic answers,
from the appeals of powerful but shallow rhetoric
and from the tribalism that demands uniformity at the cost
    of creativity,
that by listening we may learn to cherish the insight of others,
and through openness may grow in wisdom and understanding,
through Jesus Christ our Lord.

Open-mindedness – civility

Lord, we pray for your world. In a society that seems increasingly
callous and unsympathetic to the effects of our actions on others,
we pray for a return to civility in our public life, for reason and
gentleness in political discourse, for accuracy and balance in
journalism and for consideration and sensitivity in personal and
online relationships.

God of compassion,
your Son experienced the consequences of others' indifference
and the pain that comes when we allow ourselves to despise those
    with whom we disagree.
Be, this day, with all who suffer the violence of unkind actions
    and malicious words,
that they would remain steadfast in what they believe to be for the
    good of all,
and transform our society, that we may listen to one another
    in respect
and debate our shared future with thoughtfulness and good faith,
through the one who taught us that it is only the truth that shall
    set us free,
even Jesus Christ our Lord.

Open-mindedness – generosity of heart

Lord, we pray for peace in our world, for greater understanding
between people of different faiths and cultures, for renewed
efforts to find diplomatic solutions to political conflicts and for a
deeper respect for the dignity and worth of each individual human
life.

God our Creator,
who formed us to be together as one human family
and who longs for us to live in peace and fellowship with
    our neighbours,
send on all the peoples of this earth the power of your
    transforming Spirit,
that we may be open to honouring the perspectives of others,
generous in responding to their needs and weaknesses
and that we may delight to see, in the faces of others,
the features of Jesus Christ our Lord.

Open-mindedness – respect for those with intellectual disabilities

Lord, we pray for your world. We remember especially today all those living with intellectual disabilities, giving thanks for the contribution they make to our society and praying that they may be given both the support they need to live life to the full and the opportunity to teach us their wisdom.

Gracious God,
whose desire is for all people to know joy,
show us the dignity of each one of your children.
Strengthen all those who seek to support others in their
    journey of life,
and open our hearts to be challenged and informed
by voices and perspectives unlike our own,
that through the sharing of our lives
the whole world may grow
in understanding, fulfilment and love,
through Jesus Christ our Lord.

Open-mindedness – learning from one another

Lord, we pray for your world, for greater understanding of those
different from ourselves, for a renewed spirit of cooperation
and civility in public discourse, for a recognition of the wisdom
and the integrity of those with different political beliefs, and for
a spirit of laying aside personal or party advantage to serve the
common good.

O Lord, whose very being is equal love,
give us open minds to learn from one another,
open hearts to love those with whom we disagree
and open hands to serve those most in need,
that the kingdoms of this world would come to reflect more
    and more
that one kingdom of righteousness and peace,
which you have promised to us
in Jesus Christ our Lord.

Open-mindedness – teach us to be dissatisfied with the company of the like-minded

Father of all, we pray for your world, for all places where the
uncertainties of our age provoke division and discord between
neighbours, for constructive engagement with one another and
for a negotiated solution to differences. We pray for the painful
conflicts in our own country, for the courage to speak honestly to
one another of our views, the humility to accept the value of other
perspectives and for the love to recognize in one another the very
humanity that is God's greatest gift to us.

Almighty God,
whose life itself is a Trinity of love
and whose Son has called us to be one as you are one,
look with mercy on the disharmony of our world.
Encourage each one of us always to be dissatisfied with the
    company of the like-minded
and lead us to seek out other voices and new perspectives,
that through coming to experience and love our own diversity
we may grasp something of the mystery of your creation
and the glory of our creator,
through Jesus Christ our Lord.

Open-mindedness – listening to one another brings better outcomes

Lord, we pray for the life of our nation and of our world, for wisdom for our leaders, for reconciliation in our communities and for a willingness to compromise and find common purpose across our society.

God of truth,
whose will for us is greater than any one person can understand
and whose truth is broader than any one viewpoint can
    comprehend,
give us grace to acknowledge the validity of the views of others,
even when we profoundly disagree.
Show us how to value the role of every voice in finding our way
    ahead together,
that the direction of our future might be truly the shared desire of
    us all,
through Jesus Christ our Lord.

Open-mindedness – mutual respect

Lord of all creation, we pray for your world, for greater mutual
understanding and for a renewed commitment to seeking the
common good.

Heavenly Father,
you fashioned humanity to be one family,
to dwell in the delight of one another's company
and to learn from one another's wisdom,
but so often we choose the path of competition and domination.
Heal our hearts, by your gentle Spirit,
that we may come to see all people as truly our sisters and brothers,
and give to our leaders and to us all that heavenly discernment,
that we may work out ways of serving the good of each person in
   everything we do,
through Jesus Christ our Lord.

Social Harmony

Social harmony – broaden our vision

We pray for harmony in our society, for a better understanding
of our differences and for a renewed commitment to loving one
another and to deeper mutual understanding.

Lord, we thank you
that in your wisdom you chose to fashion a diverse humanity.
Keep us, we pray, from seeing too small a vision of your
   good creation,
and help us to understand the needs, desires and opinions
   of others,
that we may look on them as you do,
with eyes of love, compassion and peace,
through Jesus Christ our Lord.

Wisdom

Wisdom – (Advent: O Sapientia)

Lord, we pray for your world, that the gift of wisdom might be ever more known in our time. We pray for the leaders of the nations, that by intelligence and knowledge they may bring about a better future for their people. We pray for all those engaged in research, that through creativity and commitment they may discover new cures to disease and new inventions to lift the burdens of our lives. We pray for all who study, that they may be renewed in their enthusiasm for learning and their understanding of their subjects.

God of wisdom,
who gave us minds that we might understand all that you
    have made,
be with us as we strive to build a better future for all peoples.
Grant your Spirit of calm and reflection to our leaders,
that they may act with integrity and make decisions with truth in
    their hearts,
grant your Spirit of insight to our researchers and teachers,
that they may give good advice and discern new possibilities
    for progress,
and grant your Spirit of learning to each one of us,
that we may be open to being taught by one another,
that our knowledge may be enriched and our hearts may
    be enlarged,
in Jesus Christ our Lord.

Wisdom – knowing who to listen to

Lord, we pray for your world. Amid the difficulties and
uncertainties of our times, help us to know which voices to trust,
and grant to our leaders, the media and all whose voices gain the
attention of others, that they would speak with understanding,
truth and peace.

God of unity,
whose Son offered his life to break down the barriers of this world,
help us in our time of perplexity to hear your call.
When the way is uncertain, show us the path of truth,
when we seem trapped and lost, reveal to us the beginnings of the
    journey ahead,
and when we have gone astray, bring us back to that narrow road
where justice and peace are found,
that amid all this world's distractions,
and despite the loud voices of threat and fear,
we would be enabled to travel on,
guided by your light
and strengthened by your love,
in Jesus Christ our Lord.

Writing Your Own Collects

I was very fortunate as a fairly ignorant 17-year-old to decide, almost by chance, to apply to Balliol College, one of Oxford's most academically exciting, if not traditionally devout, establishments. Indeed, so rarely did a religious interest make itself apparent within those walls, that I am told that when a friend of mine suggested to our inspirational college chaplain that he might organize a Confirmation service for me and some others, he replied: 'I'm not sure we do that kind of thing here.' He relented, happily, and prepared us for Confirmation with a course whose only textbook was the 1662 Book of Common Prayer, and whose only homework was composing collects in the style of Dr Cranmer. Little did I realize then how useful this training would become!

The collects gathered together in this book represent a particular sort of prayer; they are far from the only way of praying. Indeed, they lack the spontaneity, intimacy and personal quality that is often thought of as the heart of an individual's spiritual life. Yet the regular shape of collects, their formal quality and their universal outlook give them the power to be heard not as the overhearing of the private prayer life of another but as the common prayer of all the souls gathered in one place, to which each voice can join its own sincere 'Amen'.

The Character of a Collect

The origin and purpose of the collect are apparent in its name: the Latin *collecta*, from the verb *colligere*, 'to collect together'. The collect gathers together the individual prayers of the people and forms them into a spiritual conclusion. Like all good conclusions, this form of prayer is brief, with a clear structure and carefully chosen language.

Brevity

Early collects are brief in the extreme. As the Roman Catholic scholar Adrian Fortescue memorably described a collect, 'it asks for one thing only and that in the tersest language' (*The Mass: A Study of the Roman Liturgy*, reprinted New York: Magisterium Press, 2015, p. 249). We might be a little more liberal – but not much. The sense of conclusion and prayerful completion is lost if the collect goes on for too long. The whole collect, therefore, needs to have the sense of being a single unified thought. Many collects are only one sentence long, although that sentence often contains two or three clauses. Even those that are more than one sentence, grammatically speaking, still have the sense of representing a single unified thought efficiently expressed.

Structure

Just as in music certain regular patterns of harmony indicate to an audience that we have come to the end of a piece, so the collect uses a fairly fixed structure to indicate that, in these words, a short time of prayer has come to a close. This regularity of structure is so familiar to many of us that we hardly notice it is there, and yet it is the key to creating the sense that the collect expresses the prayerful summation of the thoughts of many individuals.

The structure is relatively simple:

i An address to God: usually explicitly or implicitly to the Father, more rarely to the Son, even more rarely to the Spirit or to the entire Trinity. This often comes with an adjective or other brief description, e.g. *'Heavenly Father'*, *'Almighty God'*, *'God our Creator'*.

ii A mention of something God has done for us or a description of an aspect of the nature of God that is relevant for the prayer, often introduced by 'who' or 'you', e.g. *'who gave your Son that the world might have life in him'*, *'you love us with an eternal love'*.

iii A request that God does something, e.g. *'comfort all those who are in danger this day'*, *'send your love into our hearts'*. This

Writing Your Own Collects

section can be expanded a little to include a variety of related concerns, e.g. *'comfort all those who are in danger this day, help all who are in need, and bring your healing to the sick'*.

iv An indication of the desired outcome of the request that has been made, often introduced by 'that' or 'so that', e.g. *'so that all people may dwell in peace'*, *'that we may know you more deeply each day'*, *'that our nation may be a place of hospitality for all those who are drawn to this land'*.

v A conclusion, most often *'through Jesus Christ our Lord'* or similar words. If the prayer is addressed to the Son a Trinitarian ending is sometimes used, e.g. *'who lives and reigns with the Father and the Holy Spirit, one God, now and for ever'*. These formulaic endings may seem repetitive, but they are crucial because they are familiar to the congregation and allow them to pronounce their 'Amen' with confidence. It prevents the awkward pause and break of prayerful concentration caused when those gathered are not sure if the prayer is yet over.

An example:

i God of all peoples,

ii your love stretches beyond all ages
and your care extends beyond all space.

iii Bring your healing, we pray, to the fractures of this broken world.
Bind up what is wounded in our societies and in our hearts,
and renew our spirits,

iv that we may find delight in difference
and refreshment in those who are unlike us,

v through Jesus Christ our Lord.

It is, of course, possible to adapt this formula to produce a range of effects. Nevertheless, keeping to this general shape helps to give unity to the prayer, and assists the congregation by allowing them to concentrate on the contents of the prayer rather than the novelty of its construction.

Style

Each writer is likely to have their own preferred vocabulary and stylistic tendencies, but the topics mentioned below might be worthy of consideration by those beginning to write collects. The real test, though, for a collect, as for any oral form, is to read the prayer out aloud, to check it sounds clear, balanced and fluent.

Variety of vocabulary: just as in a sentence, the same word should only be repeated in a collect if there is a good reason to do so. A deliberate repetition can have a powerful effect (e.g. 'help us to know *peace* in our hearts, *peace* in our relationships and *peace* in our world'), but a chance repetition tends to sound 'clunky' and detracts from the forward motion of the prayer. The use of a synonym is better.

> Compare 'God of wisdom, who made all the earth, grant *wisdom* to your people, that ...'

> to 'God of wisdom, who made all the earth, grant *insight* to your people, that ...'.

Language patterns: a number of rhetorical features, which we have learnt to appreciate through their common use, can help the congregation to navigate and absorb the prayer.

Tricolon: the tricolon (arrangement of language in threes) is one of the most powerful and natural patterns to use. The threefold pattern is expected, and therefore gives a sense of completeness to the thought when used:

> ... and in all things grant us *love, compassion* and *peace.*

The tricolon can also be used to structure larger sections of the prayer:

> Strengthen *us in* courage, *that we* may fight injustice,
> sustain *us in* hope, *that we* may work for a better world
> and deepen *us in* love, *that we* may show kindness to all those
> we meet.

Writing Your Own Collects

As this example demonstrates, when the tricolon is used across a larger section of the prayer, it is advantageous to mark its presence by a repeated clausal structure (in this case '... *us in* ... , *that we may* ...').

Anaphora: beginning a series of clauses with the same word(s) is an effective way of giving structure to the prayer, and encourages the congregation to notice the connections between different aspects of the collect:

> *open our* eyes to the injustices of this world,
> *open our* ears to the cries of those in need,
> *open our* hearts to the sufferings of our neighbours
> and *open our* hands to serve them in our lives.

Here the repeated opening of each line builds up the sense of the huge amount of need there is in our world and, through the shifting focus on different parts of our bodies, the necessity to offer our whole selves in service.

This example is also an instance where the tricolon is being used, and adapted, to help emphasize the point of the prayer. The first three lines seem to complete the expected threefold pattern – and in terms of content they demand little more of us than to be well disposed – but the 'extra' fourth phrase comes as a surprise: we are challenged to make a response ourselves. The unexpected extension of the neat and tidy tricolon underlines the point that we need to break out of our complacency and not only pray but act. Breaking from expectations in this way can be very effective, but only if done in moderation.

Balanced and parallel phrases: Hebrew poetry, as seen in the Psalms, is structured around repetition. An idea is put forward in the first half of the verse and then often repeated or reflected on with different vocabulary in the second half, e.g. 'Your word is a *lamp to my feet* and a *light to my path*' (Psalm 119.105). This kind of repetition or development of an idea with different vocabulary works effectively in collects as well.

Lord of all,
you made us for peace, yet we have chosen war,
you made us for love, yet we have chosen hate ...
... give us wisdom in our deliberations and courage in
 our actions ...
... inspire us with hope and give us your peace ...

The balance between the phrases gives a sense of poise and completeness to the prayer and helps it to sink into the hearts of the congregation through the repetition of the idea.

Unusual word order: changing the standard word order of a sentence is an effective way of putting emphasis on a particular phrase. The most common way of doing this is to bring an adverbial phrase forwards, to stand at the head of a clause. For example:

Normal speech: '... grant us your grace, that we may serve our neighbours, our society and our world with kind and generous hearts.'

Changed word order:

 ... grant us your grace,
 that *with kind and generous hearts*
 we may serve our neighbours, our society and our world.

In the second example, the unusual word order throws emphasis on to the *'kind and generous hearts'*, inviting those at prayer to consider how we might behave in this way in each of the contexts named in the following line.

Other rhetorical techniques that tend not to figure so large in everyday speech need to be used judiciously. A gentle use of alliteration/assonance (repetition of sounds) can help to give emphasis to a point (e.g. 'keep us from the *cruelties* of *corruption*'), as can a striking use of imagery (e.g. 'that our *lives* may become one *joyful song of praise* to you'). However, devices such as these need to be used sparingly, otherwise the style of the prayer will sound contrived, ostentatious and distracting. For a similar reason, it is

Writing Your Own Collects

worth avoiding any deliberate use of rhyme, and eliminating any unintentional rhymes that lead to 'jingles', e.g. *in your light, give us sight*. In general, the objective is to produce a prayer that has been carefully crafted to sound utterly natural.

Once again, the ultimate test is to read the finished collect out loud and see how it sounds. Is it easy to read, or are there combinations of words or complexities of grammar that trip the reader up? Is it easy to understand, and does it sound like a prayer rather than a performance?

Concluding Texts

The Lord's Prayer

Traditional

Our Father, who art in heaven,
hallowed be thy name;
thy kingdom come;
thy will be done;
on earth as it is in heaven.
Give us this day our daily bread.
And forgive us our trespasses,
as we forgive those who trespass
   against us.
And lead us not into temptation;
but deliver us from evil.
For thine is the kingdom,
the power and the glory,
for ever and ever.
Amen.

Contemporary

Our Father in heaven,
hallowed be your name,
your kingdom come,
your will be done,
on earth as in heaven.
Give us today our daily bread.
Forgive us our sins
as we forgive those who sin
   against us.
Lead us not into temptation
but deliver us from evil.
For the kingdom, the power
and the glory are yours
now and for ever.
Amen.

The Grace

The grace of our Lord Jesus Christ,
and the love of God,
and the fellowship of the Holy Spirit
be with us all evermore. Amen.

Blessing

When pronounced by a priest, the 'you' form should be used as printed in the text. A layperson should use the word 'us' instead and add the word 'may' at the start.

The peace of God,
which passes all understanding,
keep your hearts and minds
in the knowledge and love of God,
and of his Son Jesus Christ our Lord;
and the blessing of God almighty,
the Father, the Son and the Holy Spirit,
be among you and remain with you always. Amen.

Common Worship: Services and Prayers for the Church of England
© The Archbishops' Council 2000.

Seasonal Blessings

Advent

Christ the Sun of Righteousness shine upon you,
scatter the darkness from before your path,
and make you ready to meet him when he comes in glory;
and the blessing ...

Christmas

May the joy of the angels,
the eagerness of the shepherds,
the perseverance of the wise men,
the obedience of Joseph and Mary,
and the peace of the Christ-child
be yours this Christmas;
and the blessing ...

Epiphany

The Lord Jesus Christ,
Son of the living God,
teach you to walk in his way more trustfully,
to accept his truth more faithfully,
and to share his life more lovingly;
that by the power of the Holy Spirit
you may come as one family to the kingdom of the Father.
And the blessing ...

Lent

Christ give you grace to grow in holiness,
to deny yourselves, take up your cross, and follow him;
and the blessing …

Passiontide & Holy Week

Christ crucified draw you to himself,
to find in him a sure ground for faith,
a firm support for hope,
and the assurance of sins forgiven;
and the blessing …

Easter

The God of peace,
who brought again from the dead our Lord Jesus,
that great shepherd of the sheep,
through the blood of the eternal covenant,
make you perfect in every good work to do his will,
working in you that which is well-pleasing in his sight;
and the blessing …

All Saints to Advent (Christ the King)

Christ our King make you faithful and strong to do his will,
that you may reign with him in glory;
and the blessing …